A BARTHOLOMEW MAP & GUIDE

EXPLORE THE BROADS

35 WALKS SELECTED & DESCRIBED
BY JEANNE LE SURF

JOHN BARTHOLOMEW & SON LTD
EDINBURGH

British Library Cataloguing in Publication Data
Le Surf, Jeanne
Explore the Broads: 35 walks.
1. Broads, The (England) — Description
and travel — Guide Books
I. Title
914.26'1704858 DA670.N6

ISBN 0 7028 0772 9

Published and printed in Scotland 1987
by John Bartholomew & Son Ltd.,
Duncan Street, Edinburgh EH9 1TA

ISBN 0 7028 0772 9

The physical landscape of Britain is changing all the time e.g. as new tracks are made, hedges grubbed up and fields amalgamated. While every care has been taken in the preparation of this guide, John Bartholomew & Son Ltd. will not be responsible for any damage or inconvenience caused by inaccuracies.

CONTENTS

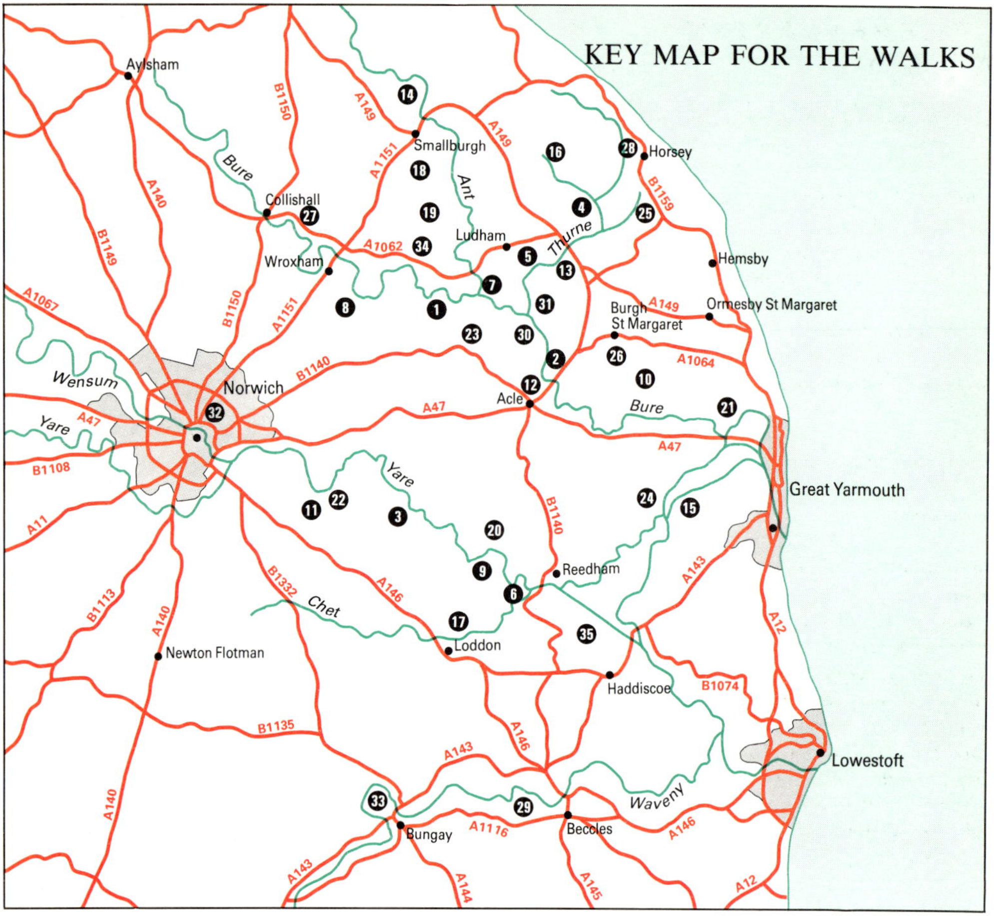

KEY MAP FOR THE WALKS

KEY TO SCALE AND MAP SYMBOLS

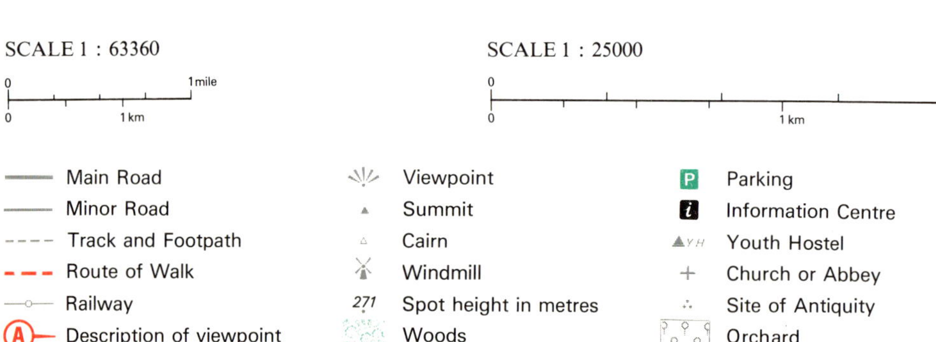

1 THE REAL ART OF WALKING

The area we call the Norfolk Broads is designated as an Area of Outstanding Natural Beauty. There are 22 Sites of Special Scientific Interest and numerous nature reserves maintained by government and voluntary societies. With such qualifications to recommend it, the committed rambler will be eager to start exploring but there are many of us who long to walk in the countryside, who would prefer some guidance on how to start.

The instinct that makes us pick up a book of walks is an indication of a deeply seated urge from our almost forgotten past. In quite recent history, the majority of us lived in the countryside. People knew and understood its sights and sounds and walked to market, church, inn and all social occasions.

From the comforts of our suburban life we have an instinct to mingle again more closely with nature.

Books of walks, such as the one you hold in your hand, provide a way to clear your doubts and set your instincts free. Firstly, it helps with important matters such as where to start and where to end: where to moor your boat or park your car and find refreshment; it explains some background to what you see and hear.

Secondly, it removes the agony of thoughts of trespass on another person's private land.

Thirdly, to go walking over farmland where others go regularly and safely is a comfort to those who fear domestic animals. There is nothing wrong with such fear, many farmers wives never cross an open field or paddock and quickly close the farmyard door when animals are in the yard. There is nothing to fear if you take notice of the simple rule to keep clear at calving time and never get between a cow and its newly born calf. Farm animals may often come crowding round but they are merely curious and can be as playful as children.

Fourthly, all wild animals will go quickly from your path and watch from a distance the dreaded human form. A fox will boldly stare then disappear in a flash as you approach. An adder basking in the sun will slide resentfully away. The only thing to fear in the British fauna is that you might tread on a wasp's nest and the determined guard of wasps come swiftly to attack. The best defence is to run away.

Finally, be assured that you are strong enough to put your best foot forward. The distance of each walk has been carefully measured. The choice of time and speed is entirely yours. A picnic, a book, a quiet spot to contemplate, to watch or rest are yours to arrange. Walking 6 miles (9.7 km) in the countryside among all its interests, is not a long way to travel when you have time to take it easy and is well within the capabilities of even those who normally lead a sedentary life.

2 ACCOMMODATION AND TOURIST INFORMATION IN THE BROADS

Tourist Information Centres:

1 The Guildhall, Norwich
Norwich 666071

2 The Quay, Fen Lane, Beccles
Beccles 713196

3 North Lodge Park, Cromer
Cromer 512497

4 The Esplanade, Lowestoft
Lowestoft 65989

The Tourist Information Centres listed above provide details of land-based holiday accommodation within the wider area of Broadland which caters for many holidaymakers in east Norfolk and north-east Suffolk. Much of the accommodation is based on higher land away from the rivers but within easy reach by car for those who do not wish to confine their visit entirely to an exploration of the Broads.

Accommodation situated nearer to the rivers and the flood plains of the Broads is available from the Tourist Information Centres in:

1 South Quay, Gt. Yarmouth
Great Yarmouth 846345

2 Station Road, Hoveton, Wroxham
Wroxham 2281

3 The Broads Authority, 18, Colegate, Norwich
Norwich 610734

You will have the choice of static caravans, chalets, flats, cottages and houseboats. The bulk of the accommodation is in Burgh Castle (Walk 15), Belton and Bradwell. All three areas are around Great Yarmouth (Walk 21).

The remainder of the accommodation is based in Stalham, Potter Heigham, Wroxham, Brundall and Oulton, all within easy access of walks in this guide.

Hand-in-hand nowadays with the straightforward provision of information which helps visitors to enjoy the Broads area to the full, centres now provide an 'interpretation of its environment'.

The Broads Authority has Information and Interpretive Centres in Ranworth Staithe (Walk 1), tel. South Walsham 453, and Beccles. They have plans for two more in future years.

The idea of interpreting the Broads for the visitor is not a new one. Voluntary societies have led the way. The Norfolk Naturalists Trust have a Visitor Centre near Ranworth Staithe (Walk 1) and another in Hickling (Walk 16), where there is also a Hickling Water Trail. The Norfolk Windmills Trust have restored a windpump in Thurne (Walks 13 and 31).

The Nature Conservancy Council has a Regional Office at 60, Bracondale, Norwich (tel. 620558), where information is available on a Nature Trail at Bure Marshes and on Sites of Special Scientific Interest (S.S.S.I.s) in Broadland. The great windpump at Berney Mill (Walk 24) is under the care of the Department of the Environment.

3 GEOGRAPHY OF THE NORFOLK BROADS AREA

The landscape which this book explores is unique in the British Isles. Wide views over a flood plain, the consistent colour but uneven texture of the grazing marsh, dykes and their fringing vegetation, the dyke gates, windpumps and bird life.

Since Victorian times, the area has been a holiday destination for those with interests in shooting, fishing and boats. The joys of boating are many but they can be increased by also walking in the surrounding areas. There are moorings near the starting places of most of these walks and car parks or other room nearby.

The Norfolk Broads covers an area of about 115 square miles (300 km^2) in the valleys of the rivers Ant, Bure, Thurne and Yare in Norfolk and, southwards, to the river Waveney which delineates the Norfolk/Suffolk border. All the rivers are publicly navigable for most of their length and there are cuts or dykes connecting with the main valley broads. Filby, Rollesby and Ormesby Broads cannot be reached from the rivers and some have been cut off from the river for environmental reasons. Of the 42 Broads, 16 are accessible and are used by sailing and power boats. There is also a limited amount of boating on those Broads not connected to the rivers.

It was shown in 1956 that the Broads were made by peat diggers sometime before the 13th century. Their excavations were on average about 13ft (4 m) deep although there were deeper workings, such as Filby Broad (Walk 26). After the 13th century, the sea level rose and flooded the workings, creating the Norfolk Broads.

A natural progression gradually infills shallow water with plant material to form a peat substrate. This is first colonised by reed swamp species and then by sedges and herbaceous plants. The next stage is the growth of alder and sallow into carr woodland and, finally, the growth of oak trees. No one knows the extent of the original water surface of the Broads but it appears from the measurement of tithe maps in 1840 that there were about 2960 acres (1200 hectares) at that time. The Broads Authority made an aerial survey in 1980 which indicated a present area of just over 1480 acres (600 hectares). Mud pumps and dredges are often at work.

In the lower reaches of the Yare and Waveney, reclaimed marshland stretches for miles with low hills, isolated farms and small areas of woodland hardly breaking the extensive views. In the upper reaches of the Ant, Bure, Yare and Thurne, the landscape is more enclosed by fen and carr woodland. The scenery is, therefore, markedly different in these two main areas of Broadland. Moreover, the interest of the observer is continually stimulated by differing ranges of plants and animals in each river, caused by the varying conditions of water flow and quality.

Management by drainage started in Norman times when banks were built to drain mud flats in the estuaries, the alluvial marshlands and the fens. This early drainage relied upon gravity, with sluices to prevent flooding during high tides.

Windpumps were introduced in the 17th century and the remains of these structures form a familiar feature on every side. By the 19th century, there were 240 working windpumps, all now redundant through the introduction of diesel and electric pumps.

The importance to commerce of the Norfolk waterways can be appreciated in an excellent display in the Maritime Museum in Great Yarmouth. A fuller emjoyment of Broadland can then be obtained by understanding the influence that trade has had upon its landscape and its riverside settlements. While exploring the area, you will see navigable dykes (Walks 9 and 12), old locks (Walk 29), pubs where Wherrymen congregated (Walks 16 and 20) and waterside buildings which were used for the storage of grain, coal, marl and ice. Perhaps you will catch a glimpse of the 'Albion', an old trading wherry under sail and the sole survivor of the scores that traded in the past.

The quay in Great Yarmouth is second in size only to Rotterdam in the European trade and fishing industry.

The Broads holiday trade began around 1860 and increased as the commerical use of the waterways declined. Between the world wars, most holiday craft were under sail but today the motor cruiser is pre-eminent.

4 HISTORY

In Roman times, the area between Caistor and Burgh, near Great Yarmouth, was a wide estuary. Through it, the earliest traders sailed, past the settlement called Norvic at the confluence of the Yare and Wensum to the Roman port of Venta Icenorum, now Caistor St. Edmund.

The Broads did not exist: only a great bay called Gariensis on which, no doubt, the Romans kept a galley or two against the northern pirates. Inside the fortifications of Burgh and its opposite arm in Caistor, rested the Dalamation Cavalry commanded by 'The Count of the Saxon Shore'.

With the departure of the Romans and the attempt by St. Augustine to extend the Christian Church beyond the border of Kent, a wandering Irish Monk, named Fursey, built a monastery within the walls of Burgh Castle (Walk 15). He was a man of apocalyptic vision, of whom Palgrave said, 'His spark kindled the first metrical compositions from whose combinations the *Divinia Commedia* of Dante arose'.

The inland rivers were then deeper and wider, frequently flooding the low plain between the higher ground until the movement of the sea tides built a long low bank of sand across the Yarmouth estuary. Islets or 'holms' were then formed inland on which the Anglo-Saxons settled as fishermen and fowlers and, later, as farmers when, by means of banks and sluices, they drained the land.

On one of these holms lived a hermit named Suneman, the earliest known inhabitant of Broadland. The Abbey of St. Benet at Holm was founded here before the Norman conquest and was one of Britain's richest abbeys (Walk 7).

The invasions and settlements of the Danes is still recorded with the suffix 'by' in villages like Filby (Walk 10) and Oby (Walk 2). All through the 9th century, the Danes ravaged the Broadland rivers until peace was made under Alfred and religious life and learning was restored. By the Middle Ages, monastries and religious houses were numerous in the Broads area (Walks 7 and 9).

From Norman times, traders have penetrated Norfolk through its Broadland rivers. Norwich Cathedral was built using Caen stone, brought to Norwich and taken through Pulls Ferry (Walk 32) to the site. Since then, the history of Broadland has been closely related to the trade upon its rivers.

The rivers rise and enter the sea within the county itself and because the contours are low, they are slow, full and safe for small craft. The continental ships that are seen following the Yare to Norwich are small enough for the canal system of northern Europe and they trade directly into inland ports as they have done for 1000 years.

On the sand bank that sealed off Gariensis, Great Yarmouth started its life as a fishing settlement and, in the middle ages, when wool was building the prosperity of Norfolk, the town expanded into a great port where goods were shipped to foreign parts.

Most Broadland villages were deliberately sited on the inland waterway system and have their own staithes as shown in several of the walks. The expansion of canal building also stretched into Norfolk and navigation was extended from Coltishall (Walk 27) to Aylsham through five locks over nine miles (14 km). A North Walsham canal was also dug but neither survived the coming of the railways. The village inn in Geldeston, which has a long cut from the Waveney to its staithe (Walk 29), is still called 'The Wherry'.

5 THE ENVIRONMENT OF THE BROADS

In 1986, when the government realised that the Norfolk Broads were in danger of decline, a Broads Bill was introduced into parliament. The Bill spells out the necessary maintenance of the Broads. With commendable speed, Broadland was also designated an Environmentally Sensitive Area under section 41 of the Wildlife and Countryside Act of 1981, whereby owners can manage the grazing marshes in the traditional way.

The traditional landscape is secured between the Bure and the Yare, from Upton and South Walsham Marshes (Walk 30) to Halvergate (Walk 24) and through to Great Yarmouth (Walk 15), then to the south side of the Waveney between Beccles (Walk 29) and Lowestoft. Indeed, an area near the Berney Mill (Walk 24) will be purposely flooded, for part of the year, by the Norfolk Naturalists Trust in order to attract wild fowl in the same numbers as they were before modern drainage began.

In summer, populations of mute swan, shoveller, oyster catcher, lapwing, redshank and yellow wagtail nest on the sides of the dykes or in grassy tussocks. Mallard, teal, gadwall and shelduck graze upon the grass, while waders like Avocet, many sorts of sandpiper and temminks stint, feed as passage migrants upon invertebrates in the shallows.

In the winter months, the marshes provide a feeding and roosting area for over-wintering waders and wildfowl, including bean geese, bewick and mute swans, widgeon, golden plover, snipe, golden eye, pintail, pochard and the tufted duck. When the weather is hard, mergansers and gooseanders fly in.

With the spring, passage migrants come: osprey, spoonbill and black tern. Closely observing the marsh, predators include the kestrel, marsh and hen harriers which contrast with the awkwardly flapping heron and cormorant. At night, the barn and the short-eared owl appear. Migrant visitors are the Montague harrier and the great grey shrike.

Among the reedbeds and carr woodland are woodpeckers and jays, the reed and sedge warblers and, occasionally, a bearded tit. The greylag and Canada geese with the green sandpiper may also occasionally appear. Bobbing on the rivers are coots, grebes and water rail and there are occasional flights of common tern. Sometimes a bittern will be heard to boom. Both the recently identified Savis and Cetti's warbler breed on Hickling (Walk 16).

In these areas of level fields, formed before the 18th century and used for summer pasture, there is a complex system of drains and dykes through which water flows to the pumps. Here is the heart of Broadland which has retained all the plants and most of the related animals which are known to this environment. A total of 108 aquatic plant species have been recorded as well as many populations of aquatic invertebrates, including the rare Aeshna dragonfly. Traditional management as grazing marsh keeps the water table at a high level and regularly cleans the dykes, thereby ensuring a sufficient depth for plant growth.

Farm animals also help by regularly grazing along the banks and this prevents the growth of long grass and shrubs which might shut out the light. On the edge of the marshes, near the higher ground, where they are fed by fresh spring water, there are dykes of more ecological importance. These feature in walks around Ludham (Walks 5 and 7), Potter Heigham (Walks 4 and 13), Upton (Walks 12 and 30), Cantley (Walk 20) and Dilham (Walk 14). Lilies, water soldier and uncommon plants can be found, including lesser tussock sedge, black bog rush, round-leaved wintergreen and marsh fern.

Wet areas in the first stage of the succession from open water to carr woodland are called fens. In areas where the water is of good quality, there are quantities of sphagnum moss and a wide range of plant species including rarities, such as the fen orchid and the crested buckler fern. All these wonders depend upon a management policy that includes the cutting of reeds, which can be sold, and marsh hay, which cannot. The Broads Authority are making an economic job of reed harvesting at How Hill and Horsey. They are also clearing the dykes by transporting the reed along them as it was traditionally done in the past. The cutting of peat has also been tried and many species have returned. The spectacular swallowtail butterfly feeds here on the milk parsley found in fens among marsh thistles, yellow iris, angelica and hemp agrimony. Among the sedge beds are bog myrtle and creeping willow together with many orchids such as the early marsh, southern marsh, marsh helleborine and lesser butterfly orchid. In the Upton Fen Reserve (Walk 23), rare plants include the lesser tussock sedge, black bog rush, round-leaved wintergreen and marsh fern. The Broads Authority are anxious to open more access to the fen areas of Broadland.

Alarm bells began to ring among the naturalists, and those who simply enjoyed the beauty of the Broads, when a green appearance was noticed in the shining waters. Surveys were made which showed that action would have to be taken.

Broadland rivers and their associated broads support a wide range of submerged and semi-submerged water plants known as macrophytes. These plants are the base of the aquatic food chain which gives food and shelter for a great variety of insects and small aquatic animal life.

The green appearance was a rapid growth of algae. An increase of phosphates from the public sewers into the rivers, together with nitrates from the agricultural run-off, were enriching the water into a strongly fertile medium. The result was a choking of the macrophytes by the enveloping algae. Among the remedies now in use, in the war of the great reversal, are phosphate strippers on the sewage pumping plants and an agreement with farmers to abandon high-input farming and a return to traditional management. Only four out of the 42 broads were completely unaffected because they were not connected to the main rivers. They were also surrounded by fen which filtered out the enriching nutrients. Acting on this, the Broads Authority shut Cockshoot Broad off from the river with dramatic results. A biological approach was also made with the introduction of water fleas that eat the algae.

The river banks and the ronds, where rosebay, willowherb, yellow iris and dogrose bloom among reeds and sedges, are suffering erosion by a wash from passing boats. Their replacement by steel piling would be an act of expensive vandalism causing the Broadland rivers to look like continental canals. There is a search for an ideal boat hull that would cause a minimum height of bow wave. It cannot be doubted that the new move will succeed. Meanwhile, the eroded parts of the bank are enclosed by chestnut palings. An ingenious system of natural regeneration is being encouraged that detracts not a jot from the visual aspect of these lovely places.

Further reading:
Broadland Adventure, J. Wentworth Day. E P Publishing Ltd., (Wakefield), 1976. 2nd ed.

6 PUBLIC RIGHTS OF WAY

Public footpaths are by far the most interesting means to see and explore Broadland. Many of the paths used in this book are the routes our forefathers used when going about their daily business. They lead to windpumps, public staithes, riverside tow paths; to inns, villages and market places; through woods, across farmland and fields. From the busiest to the loneliest places, they are woven into the life of this historic and thriving countryside.

As the paths came into being to meet local needs, so has the law evolved to resolve the conflicts of interest that inevitably arose. All the paths used in these walks are public rights of way, protected by the Highways Act of 1980 and affected by the provisions of the Wildlife and Countryside Act 1981. It is most unlikely that you will meet with anything but courtesy upon them.

These paths have all been taken from the Norfolk Definitive Map and their line most carefully followed. No one can interfere with the right to use these green ways, even if it is claimed that their inclusion on the map was wrong.

If a path is obstructed by water or mud, the 'founderous' section may be passed to right or left on firmer ground. Likewise, an obstruction caused by an abandoned vehicle or a deliberate obstruction with fences or gates entitles the user to choose an alternative route. It is not clear, however, if the right to by-pass may only be used over ground owned by the person who obstructed the path: anyone choosing an alternative for that reason must take care not to cause unreasonable damage.

You are entitled to walk over a ploughed field or through a cereal crop. Potatoes, kale and oil-seed rape are a different matter and are treated in law as obstructions. You should not, therefore, choose an alternative to walking through a wheat crop, such as going around the field edge, unless the farmer has left both a clear headland path and invited its use with a footpath sign. Without an invitation, you would be trespassing if you used an alternative path when an unobstructed one was available. Landowners must take reasonable steps to see that anyone lawfully entering their land can do so safely. To enter on a public footpath is a lawful act but using the edges of fields is a trespass unless there is an invitation to do so and the user could be outside the owner's duty of care.

There is no public let to wander at will in Broadland. Users are confined to the public network of rights of way which are available to, walkers on footpaths, horse-riders, cyclists, ramblers on bridleways and all traffic on carriageways as far as they are able.

The maintenance of most public rights of way is the responsibility of the Highway Authority which is responsible for clearing obstructions and cutting away the undergrowth. The task in Broadland on the riverside paths is a colossal one and the walker must always be prepared for a tangled section. It is, at first sight, an oddity of law that anyone on a right of way may remove just enough of an obstruction in order to continue on the path but no one can go with the express intention to clear the obstruction for the general good. In the latter case, permission must be obtained from the Highway Authority, the owner informed and arrangements made to dispose of the rubbish.

The confidence to use and enjoy a public footpath is greatly helped by a signpost. It is the duty of the Highway Authority to erect a signpost wherever a footpath leaves a metalled highway, except where a parish council objects. There are a number of circular walks marked with yellow arrows (Walk 4).

A walker may take a dog 'on a lead or under close control' as a companion on a public right of way, provided that it is not 'a nuisance to other users or injurious to the soil'.

7 RESPONSIBILITIES

It was part of John Stuart Mill's philosophy that 'No one made the land, therefore, no one can own it absolutely' and it is very clear in this modern age that private ownership of great areas of countryside is tolerable only if there is some right of public access. However, it is equally important that people who live in these picturesque areas should not have, either their surroundings, or their livelihoods, damaged by enthusiastic visitors. There are a few simple things we can do to avoid inconveniencing them. All users of Broadland should close gates after them when crossing farmland and, as a rule, people should not walk more than two abreast. Avoid trespassing as far as possible and do not interfere with the work of the countryside.

Most birds and animals are now protected by the Wildlife and Countryside Act 1981 and, although the lunatic fringe seldom leave the towns or staithes, there is adequate legislation to deal with those who do scatter litter or cause damage in this marvellous landscape.

8 SAFETY

On these wide marshes, dykes are numerous, unbridged and sometimes deep. The marsh carrs and fens may be deep with bog and even the carr woodland could be dangerous underfoot. It is wise to stay on the footpaths, especially in autumn and winter when the sea scud or mist can hide every landmark in a soft wet screen. The grazing cattle are never a problem but it is quite possible to meet a bull on the marsh. Bulls have a highly unpredictable nature that requires plenty of room. The best advice is to try to remain alert and if you do see a bull, keep clear. Bulls will swim across dykes to mix with new herds of cows. They are much too busy at such times to bother with walkers but a wise rambler will swiftly depart. Few ordinary people are able to distinguish a bull of a beef breed from the more aggressive dairy bull. A beef breed bull is permitted to graze upon a public footpath but a dairy bull may not.

At times, bankside paths run close to rivers which are slow and deep aand may have an undertow. Reasonable care should be taken, especially with young children running ahead. In summer time, too, long undergrowth may cover the plank bridges over wide cuts and a false step could result in a sudden ducking. These dangers are not frequent but walkers should take reasonable care on a bank top path.

9 EQUIPMENT

Mud after rain, or walking in places where the tidal rivers flow gently on the path at high tides, make the wearing of boots or wellies more comfortable than walking shoes. The growth in high summer of luxuriant brambles among the herbage make shorts a painful choice. It is sensible, also, after rain to have waterproof trousers in your pack and, above all, to always carry a rainproof coat.

As with any trip into the countryside, it is also wise to carry with you a small first aid pack with small plasters for minor cuts, dressings for a deeper wound and triangular bandages for sprains and strains. An ointment for stings and a bottle of smelling salts could be helpful and a little warm clothing for the late afternoon when the east wind blows.

10 MAPS AND MAP READING

Maps on the 1:50,000 scale covering the Broads area are very useful. A compass with your map will help you find your way. There are no hills or gradients to complicate your timing but being able to read the symbols on a map can give a greater interest. It is also useful to find your exact location at any time should you go astray and be faced with a long and tiring extension to your journey. Always take note on your map of the direction in which you are heading so that you can return to your starting point or find the nearest road. In these wide spaces, it is easy to see the valleys, rivers and villages in the distance as you set your map to the north with your compass. You can then pick out a prominent object in the distance and, secondly, some other object in line with it but nearer to you. By identifying these two objects on your map, you then draw, or imagine, a line extending through them both. Now look in another direction at right angles to your first and pick out two more objects in the same way. Again imagine or draw a line joining these two objects and where the two lines cross on the map is where you are standing.

Without a compass, the sun can be used to find north. Remember that the sun moves from east to west and is due south at midday. Hold your watch flat so that the hour hand points to the sun (ignore the minute hand). A line halfway between the hour hand and 12 o'clock will point due south.

Take care when entering woodland that you always keep your landmarks near. A compass will help should you go astray by accident or design but woods can be quite confusing without a bearing and you might be completely lost even though only a few yards from a road.

11 BOATS

Passenger vessels:
There are about 30 passenger vessels on the Broads catering for day trips.

They are based at Hickling, Potter Heigham, Norwich, Oulton Broad, Horning, Great Yarmouth and Hoveton.

Hire vessels:
Two thirds of the motor cruisers and almost all sailing craft are based on the Thurne, Bure and Ant. Bookings are mainly organised by two letting agencies, Blakes and Hoseasons, and you can book on a day or a weekly basis. The boats cater for between two and 11 people and the season usually extends from April to October.

Full particulars can be obtained from:
Blakes Holidays Limited, Wroxham, Norfolk, or from 'Dial A Brochure' on Wroxham 3226.
Hoseasons Holidays Limited, Sunway House, 975 Oulton Broad, Lowestoft. Brochure request may be made to Lowestoft 87373.

Walk 1

RANWORTH BROAD

4 miles (6.4km) Easy; strong shoes recommended

With the help of a nature trail on this walk, you can gain more knowledge of the area and, thereby, increase your enjoyment. Moreover, you can marvel at the treasures in Ranworth Church and enjoy the panoramic view from its tower.

The name 'Ranworth' is derived from two names – rond, a name that is used to describe a strip of land on a river bank and 'worth' from an Anglo-Saxon name for estate. The 'village-by-the-river' is both poetical and accurate.

A Standing on the staithe at Ranworth, you can enjoy the view over the sparkling water to the jungle-like swampland by which it is enclosed. The view in summer includes scores of holiday craft for whom the staithe provides shops and refreshments. The staithe has also been improved for visitors with car parks and clumps of trees but the wild view across the waters is timeless.

As you can see, this area of the Bure is bordered by large areas of unreclaimed fen. The site is one of the most important wetland areas in Britain where we can find bog myrtle, ancient tussock sedges, the rare marsh and the Royal ferns.

The Swallow-tail butterfly is the largest in England and finds its food in the milk parsley which grows in the open area of the fen. This brilliant creature can be frequently seen on summer days as it flaps vigorously then soars and glides over a short distance. It is unique to the Norfolk Broads and Ranworth is its breeding ground.

The great crested grebe, the coot and, of course, the graceful swan will be seen upon the waters. In summer, the common tern breeds upon a specially designed raft on the Broad.

B Nearing the end of this path, South Walsham Broad comes into view on your left.

C From the moment of entering the church, it is immediately clear that great wealth was poured into the building and furnishing of this 'Cathedral of the Broads', as it is often called. The parish was closely connected with the wool industry in the middle ages and the great prosperity that it brought.

Norfolk benefitted from its good sheep farming country. Equally important was the transport system provided by the great rivers, Bure, Yare, Waveney with all their tributaries and the lesser rivers like the Ant and Wensum. Trade with other areas in Britain and abroad prospered.

Englishmen in those days built and beautified churches in the belief that God had made them prosperous. Though much of the magnificance has gone from Ranworth, sufficient remains for us to put together an idea of its splendour: the damaged screen, the font, the lovely chancel.

The blame for the desecration of churches is placed upon the Puritans but that is not entirely true. Most of the damage to the magnificent screen in Ranworth was done in Tudor times when hatred of the church began.

The original paint has been uncovered and cleaned by experts and the screen closely approaches its appearance in olden times. It is one of the finest in England.

Under a baize cloth, in a glass case nearby, there is an illuminated book with 285 sheepskin pages containing, in mediaeval latin, the services for every day of the year.

It is also possible to climb the tower and from 96 feet (29.3m), a glorious view of Broadland is obtained.

D There is a nature trail on the edge of the Broad leading to a Conservation Centre run by the Norfolk Naturalists Trust. Here you can learn about the shrinking and changing nature of Broadland: how the reeds decay into peat and become swamp carr, then progress into alder carr. The final act in the tragedy of a lost Broad comes when the alder carr becomes firm ground where oak trees grow.

Over

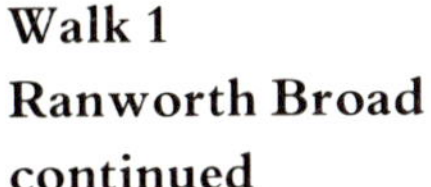

Walk 1
Ranworth Broad
continued

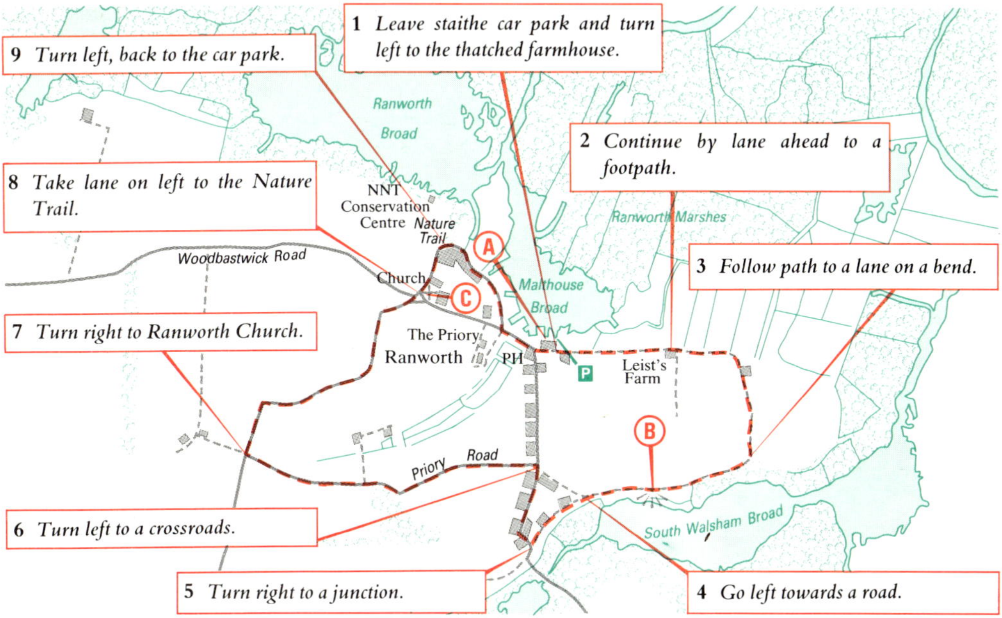

1 *Leave staithe car park and turn left to the thatched farmhouse.*

2 *Continue by lane ahead to a footpath.*

3 *Follow path to a lane on a bend.*

4 *Go left towards a road.*

5 *Turn right to a junction.*

6 *Turn left to a crossroads.*

7 *Turn right to Ranworth Church.*

8 *Take lane on left to the Nature Trail.*

9 *Turn left, back to the car park.*

Walk 2

ACLE AND MUCK FLEET

7 miles (11.3km) Moderate; strong shoes recommended, shorts unsuitable

Cultivation had been increased in the 18th century by the introduction of windmills which operated by scooping and lifting the water up and then into the river. Electric pumps in brick sheds now perform this task and have made possible a lowering of the water table. As a result, in some places, dull cereals have replaced some of the picturesque green pastures, dotted with cattle, which made the area very attractive. The government has responded to the public outcry against the changes with the introduction of new regulations to ensure that the area is designated as an Environmentally Sensitive Area. The area's decline will be reversed and its traditional wildlife and colour will be fully restored.

The landscape's mills are redundant and lonely but they retain an air of solid worth. As we near the end of Muck Fleet (B), we can enjoy the sight of a mill converted to private use and an observatory built upon the mill's truncated cone.

A In the enormous expanse which you can see all around, stretching between Acle and the sea, we can form an impression of how much effort must have been involved in mediaeval times in building great banks and draining the marshes. This achievement drew praise in 1834 from Authur Young who said 'no country has made more progress in the enclosure, cultivation and drainage of marshes than Norfolk'.

B The Muck Fleet is a typical stream of the Broads area: slow, deep and green with weed. It once served as a drain for thousands of acres of marsh and was navigable between the Bure and the three great broads of Filby, Rollesby and Ormesby. In the comfort of summer, dragonflies dart among the waterlilies while butterflies are blown among the waving grasses.

Over

Walk 2
Acle and Muck Fleet continued

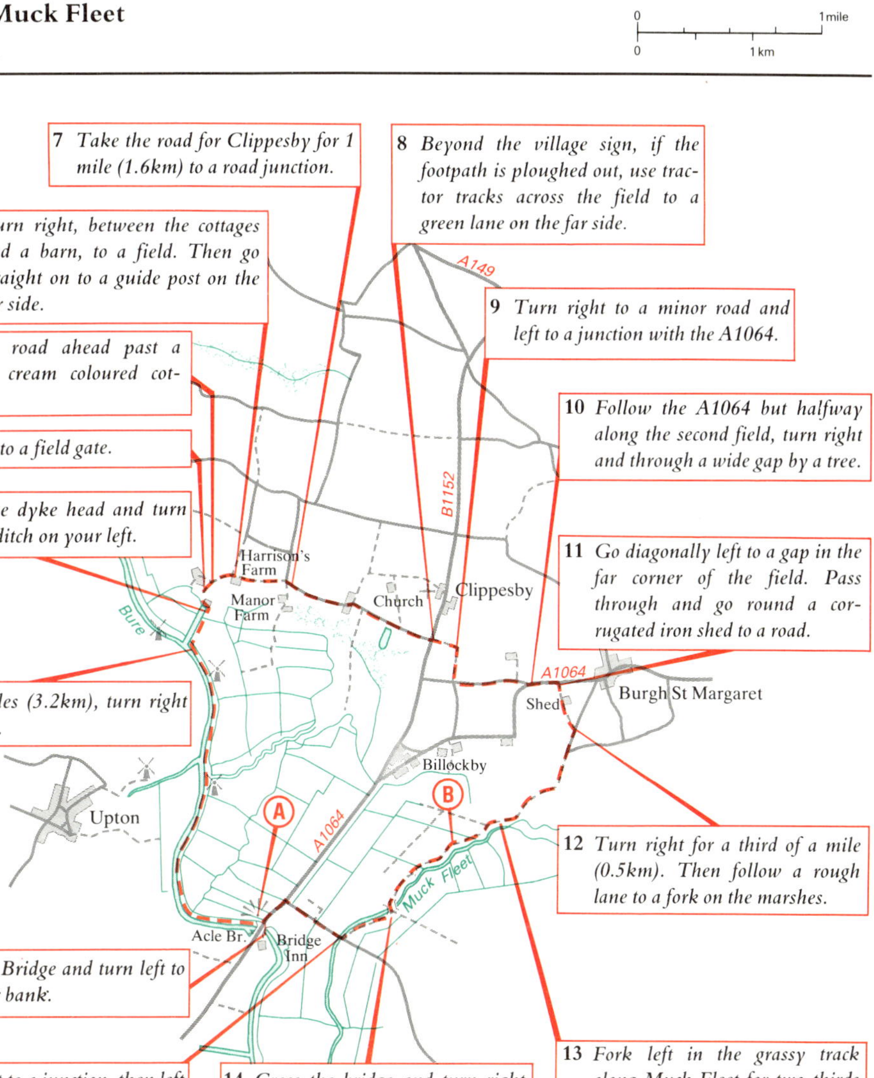

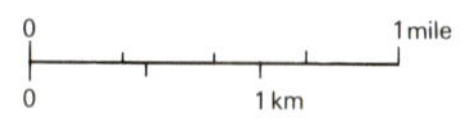

1 *Cross Acle Bridge and turn left to follow river bank.*

2 *After 2 miles (3.2km), turn right along dyke.*

3 *Go past the dyke head and turn left with a ditch on your left.*

4 *Bend right to a field gate.*

5 *Follow the road ahead past a junction to cream coloured cottages.*

6 *Turn right, between the cottages and a barn, to a field. Then go straight on to a guide post on the far side.*

7 *Take the road for Clippesby for 1 mile (1.6km) to a road junction.*

8 *Beyond the village sign, if the footpath is ploughed out, use tractor tracks across the field to a green lane on the far side.*

9 *Turn right to a minor road and left to a junction with the A1064.*

10 *Follow the A1064 but halfway along the second field, turn right and through a wide gap by a tree.*

11 *Go diagonally left to a gap in the far corner of the field. Pass through and go round a corrugated iron shed to a road.*

12 *Turn right for a third of a mile (0.5km). Then follow a rough lane to a fork on the marshes.*

13 *Fork left in the grassy track along Muck Fleet for two-thirds of a mile (1km) to a footbridge.*

14 *Cross the bridge and turn right in a track to a road.*

15 *Turn right to a junction, then left to the Bridge Inn.*

Harrison's Farm
Manor Farm
Church
Clippesby
A149
B1152
A1064
Burgh St Margaret
Shed
Billockby
Bure
Upton
A
B
Muck Fleet
Acle Br.
Bridge Inn

Walk 3

ROCKLAND BROAD

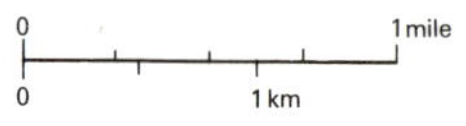

5 miles (8km) Moderately easy; strong shoes recommended

A The higher ground (by Norfolk standards) provides some very good views up to Claxton Church. Flint walls and a 14th-century tower stand on a hill girdled by trees.

B The Claxton Marsh stretches from the sedge-lined border of Rockland Broad to a road by the Beauchamp Arms. In earlier days, the publican was also a ferryman but a waterman's skill is no longer needed. The lonely pub is now a place for good refreshment. Even today, when modern machinery has made deep drainage highly efficient, there is still something primitive about these wide marshes. Great cloud masses sail over the valley and there is a feeling of space and distance.

C Rockland Broad has a path around its southeast side which, at the time of writing, is overgrown but plans are in hand to have it cleared. Until that happy day, we must walk in the adjoining meadow and climb up occasionally for a view of the gleaming water. Nevertheless, there is something deeply attractive about this lonely place.

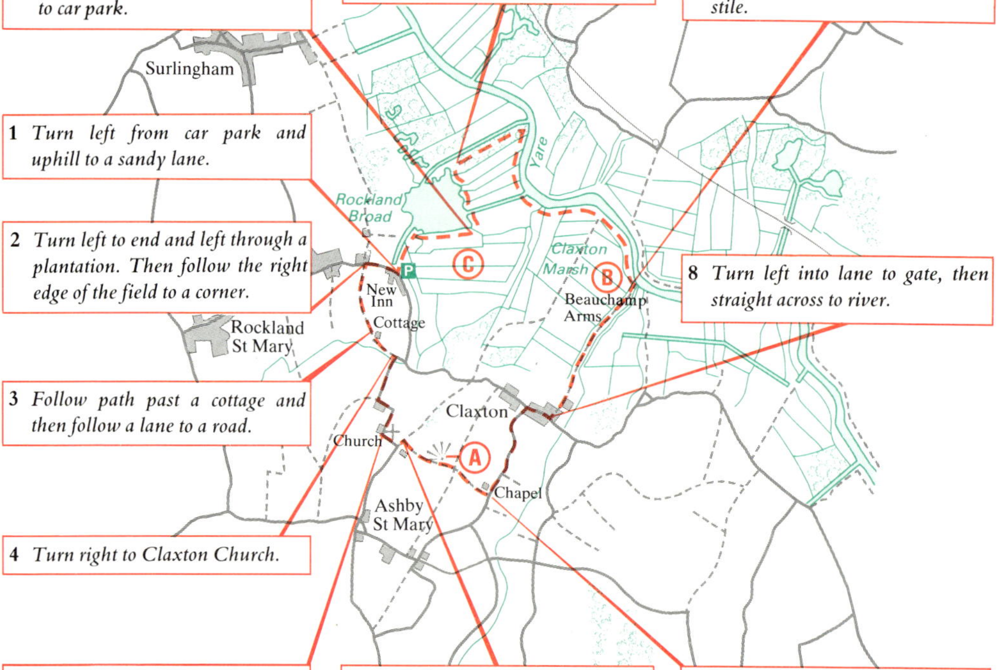

1 *Turn left from car park and uphill to a sandy lane.*

2 *Turn left to end and left through a plantation. Then follow the right edge of the field to a corner.*

3 *Follow path past a cottage and then follow a lane to a road.*

4 *Turn right to Claxton Church.*

5 *Turn left past the church down hill and left past a barn.*

6 *Turn right uphill into a track, then downhill to Baptist Chapel.*

7 *Turn left into Claxton and turn right to post box.*

8 *Turn left into lane to gate, then straight across to river.*

9 *Turn left (pub to your right) for a mile (1.6km) to dyke and left to a stile.*

10 *Go to Rockland Broad and bear left to a gate.*

11 *Pass through and turn right to another gate. Follow lane ahead to car park.*

Surlingham
Rockland Broad
Yare
Claxton Marsh
P
New Inn
Cottage
Rockland St Mary
Beauchamp Arms
Claxton
Church
Chapel
Ashby St Mary
A
B
C

Walk 4

POTTER HEIGHAM

4 miles (6.4km) Easy; strong shoes recommended, shorts unsuitable

Parking space available outside the church. Mooring in Potter Heigham village 1 mile (1.6km) away.

The Romans made tiles in Potter Heigham, where suitable clay and ready transport on the River Thurne to markets ensured the industry's prosperity into mediaeval times. A charming three-arched mediaeval bridge still survives in the town.

A We start the walk from St. Nicholas Church with its round tower and a small figure in a niche over the door of a man dressed in leaves. A 'Green Man' was an ancient fertility god and is an example of the 'belt and braces' beliefs of our ancestors who mixed their ancient gods in with the new.

B An information board erected by the Broads Authority explains the ecology of Colls Plantation. Walk through the trees to arrive at the bank surrounded by a reedy fen on the edges of the largest open water in Broadland.

Hickling Broad, Heigham Sound and the White Slea cover more than a square mile of wild country. On all sides are tasselled reed, reed mace and sedge and, occasionally the flash and gleam of miniature broads where coot and ducks congregate.

C Wagonhill Plantation is a bird sanctuary owned by the Norfolk Naturalists Trust. Woodland, the extensive reed beds and nearby grazing marsh are most important for wildlife. That is why this is a Ramsar Convention site.

Wildfowl winter in this area, particularly the Bewick and Whooper swans and you might also see a marsh harrier or a goosander. In summer, terns and warblers frequent the Broad and passage migrants include the osprey, spoonbill and the great grey shrike.

D Sound Plantation has a heronry high in its tree tops. For the birdwatching enthusiast, summer visitors here include Savi's and Cetti's warblers.

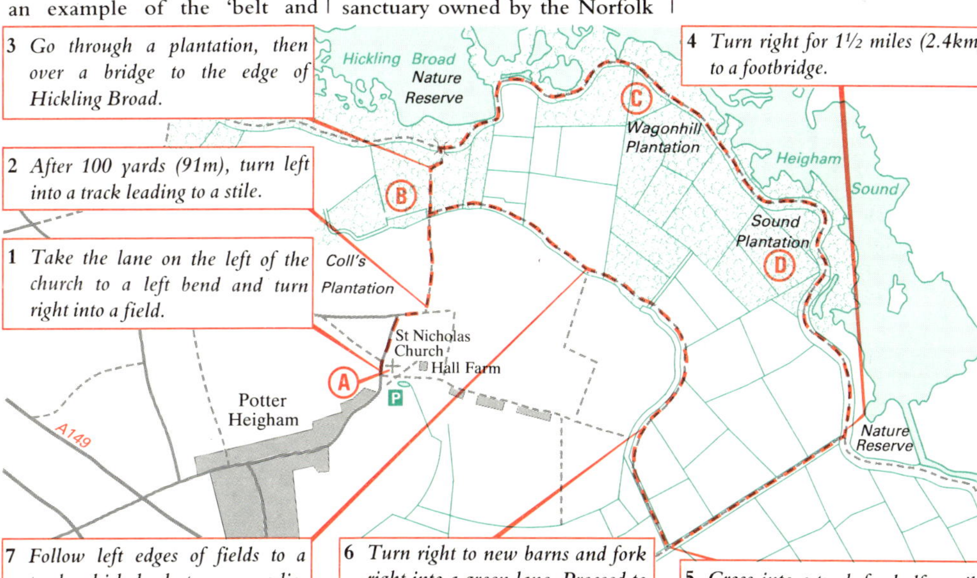

1 *Take the lane on the left of the church to a left bend and turn right into a field.*

2 *After 100 yards (91m), turn left into a track leading to a stile.*

3 *Go through a plantation, then over a bridge to the edge of Hickling Broad.*

4 *Turn right for 1½ miles (2.4km) to a footbridge.*

5 *Cross into a track for half a mile (0.8km) to a junction opposite a windmill.*

6 *Turn right to new barns and fork right into a green lane. Proceed to its end, then along the left edge of a wood to a footbridge.*

7 *Follow left edges of fields to a track which leads to your earlier path and back to the church.*

Walk 5
WOMACK WATER
3 miles (4.8km) Easy

Adequate car parking and mooring on the bank at Womack Staithe.

A In the lane from Womack Staithe to Womack Water, there is a specimen of the Giant Hogweed which is at least 12ft (3.6m) tall. The species has escaped from gardens where it was recently introduced and is rapidly spreading near streams and roads. Thus, we will see it on this route by the River Thurne and in Old Mill Lane. The stems are up to 3 inches (8cm) in diameter and are a temptation to children who may use them for telescopes or blowpipes. The juice can, however, cause severe blistering when the skin has been exposed to sunlight.

Flower arrangers are quite fond of the dried stems and fruits for giant flower displays but the plant must be thoroughly dried before taking indoors because its strong smell becomes almost overpowering.

B This mile along the Thurne, accompanied by reed buntings and sedge warblers, is a pure Broadland delight. Yellow iris, rosebay and dogrose decorate the bank and the waving reed beds. On the river, craft under sail glide smoothly to the smack of shrouds and rapidly shaking sails making good or poor progress according to the skill of the helmsman.

C The focal point of the walk from its approach along the smooth Thurne is Ludham Marsh. It is now under the control of the Nature Conservancy Council who are endeavouring to restore its traditional life and usage. The dykes abound with aquatic plants and small animals, including a rare Norfolk Aestina dragonfly. Many species, including snipe and redshank, frequent the Reserve.

Summer grazing manages the grassland and the dykes are treated by 'slubbing' in an effort to remove excess nitrates and algae growth so that the water may be less poisonous to plant growth.

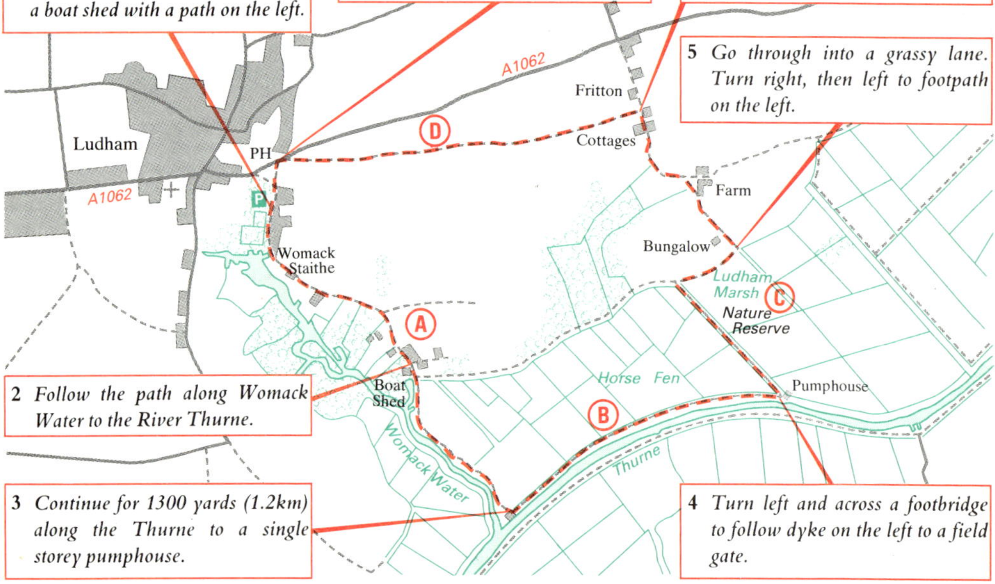

1 *Leaving the car park on Womack Staithe in Ludham, turn right to a boat shed with a path on the left.*

2 *Follow the path along Womack Water to the River Thurne.*

3 *Continue for 1300 yards (1.2km) along the Thurne to a single storey pumphouse.*

4 *Turn left and across a footbridge to follow dyke on the left to a field gate.*

5 *Go through into a grassy lane. Turn right, then left to footpath on the left.*

6 *Follow the footpath, then a lane to a road.*

7 *Turn left and left again to Womack Water.*

Walk 6

HARDLEY CROSS

4 miles (6.4km) Easy; strong shoes recommended, shorts unsuitable

Motorists can start this walk from the church at (1), boat users from the staithe at (2).

A In the days before MacAdam, Norfolk was easily accessible by water and its earlier settlers from Stone Age men to the Danes were able to penetrate inland on the rivers that flowed here through Broadland.

In later centuries, Norfolk's prosperity was based on the ease with which goods and commodities were moved by its waterways between manufacturers in Norwich and Yarmouth port.

Inevitably, there was conflict: Yarmouth stood astride the rivers that flowed to the east so that all trade between Norwich and the European mainland passed through the Yarmouth port. In the Middle Ages, at the busy Yarmouth Quay, ships cargo was loaded and transported to the wherries which took it to Norwich. Yarmouth Quay was the second largest port in Europe. Wool and woollen goods were taken down river to be loaded into strong little ships bound for continental and even Mediterranean ports. Yarmouth grew rich on the cargoes that crossed its quay.

After many disputes, a cross was erected in 1543 where the River Chet met the Yare at Hardley to mark the boundary where Yarmouth authority over navigation ended and the authority of Norwich began.

Each year, until recently, citizens from the port met those from Norwich and made a proclamation invoking peace and prosperity for all. Then, as was the custom in those uninhibited days, they went on with high jinks and water frolics.

With the great increase in trade by the 19th century, the New Cut (Walk 15) was built in order to connect Norwich directly to the sea through Lowestoft. The importance of the New Cut was soon defeated by the advent of the railways.

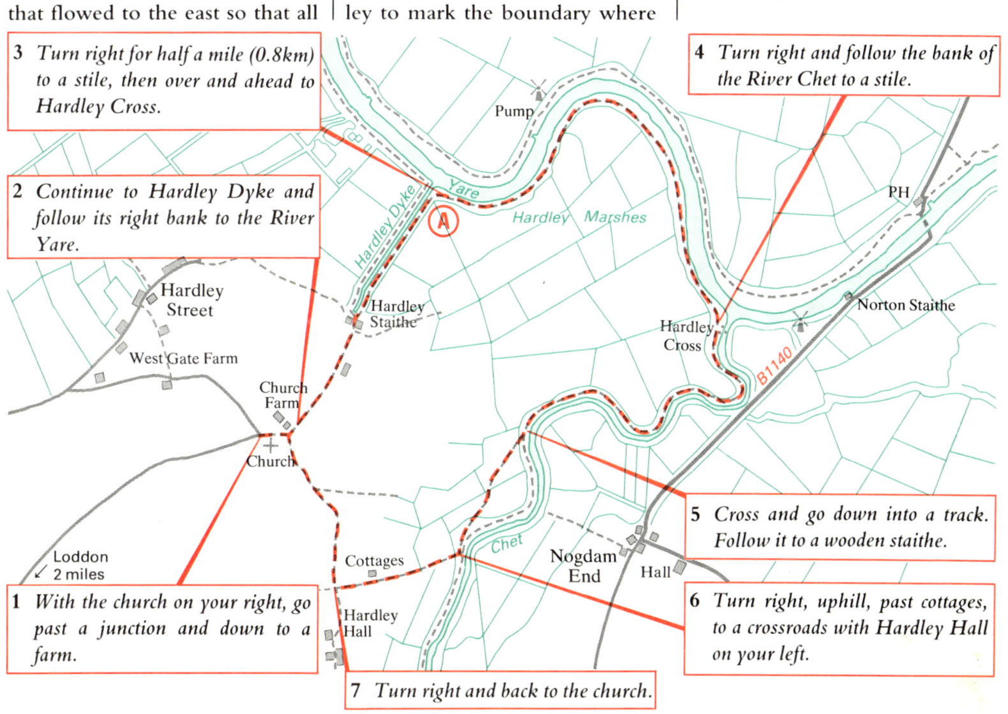

Walk 7

LUDHAM AND ST. BENET'S ABBEY

5 miles (8km) Easy; shorts unsuitable

There is adequate car parking and free mooring at Womack Staithe (1).

A Ludham is an attractive Broadland town with some attractive 18th-century houses and a splendidly sited church. The fine East Window has a quatre-foil tracery which has been most beautifully worked.

B St. Benet's Abbey provides the great interest in this walk. Situated near the Bure on a small island, it was once surrounded by great fens and marsh.

These small islands, or 'holms' as they were called by Anglo-Saxons, were the dwelling places of fishermen and fowlers. Suneman, the first known inhabitant of Broadland, lived here as a hermit. Later, Canute established the rich Abbey of St. Benet at Holm. From here it over-lorded the whole of the River Bure. The embankment of the River Ant was completed by 1274 and we can see as we walk along how it protected the lands of St. Benet.

A story is told that the Abbey withstood William the Conqueror for many years until access to its causeway was betrayed by a treacherous monk. Accepting a promise that he would be made Abbot of St. Benet's, he led the Normans over the marshes into the defended area. With grim Norman humour, William made the monk Abbot of St. Benet's and, with equal ceremony, hanged him from the Abbey gateway.

The Abbey was the only monastery not dissolved by Henry VIII who united it with Norwich. The present Bishop of Norwich sits in the Lords with the title of Abbot of St. Benet at Holm. On the Late Summer Holiday every year, the Bishop, in full regalia, arrives on a wherry and conducts a service for holiday makers under the Abbey gateway.

You will pass the great fish ponds as you walk to the gaunt remains of what was once a great Principality. All that remains are the fragments of a once mighty cruciform church in which Sir John Falstaff lies buried. He was a great knight of Henry V who fought at Agincourt and became Governor of Anjou and Maine. He was unjustly branded a coward after his troops fled in disorder at Pateye before the legendary Joan of Arc whom they believed had magical powers. Later he was caricatured by Shakespeare.

Thurne Church lies 1½ miles (2.4km) to the east of St. Benet's and, in its tower, there is a small opening looking directly across the marsh to the monastery. In the days of the monks, a light would be placed at the opening indicating that assistance was needed for a sick person. The monks, according to their charitable calling, would obey the light and bring whatever healing remedies they had to relieve and succour the distressed.

Over

Walk 7
Ludham and St. Benet's Abbey continued

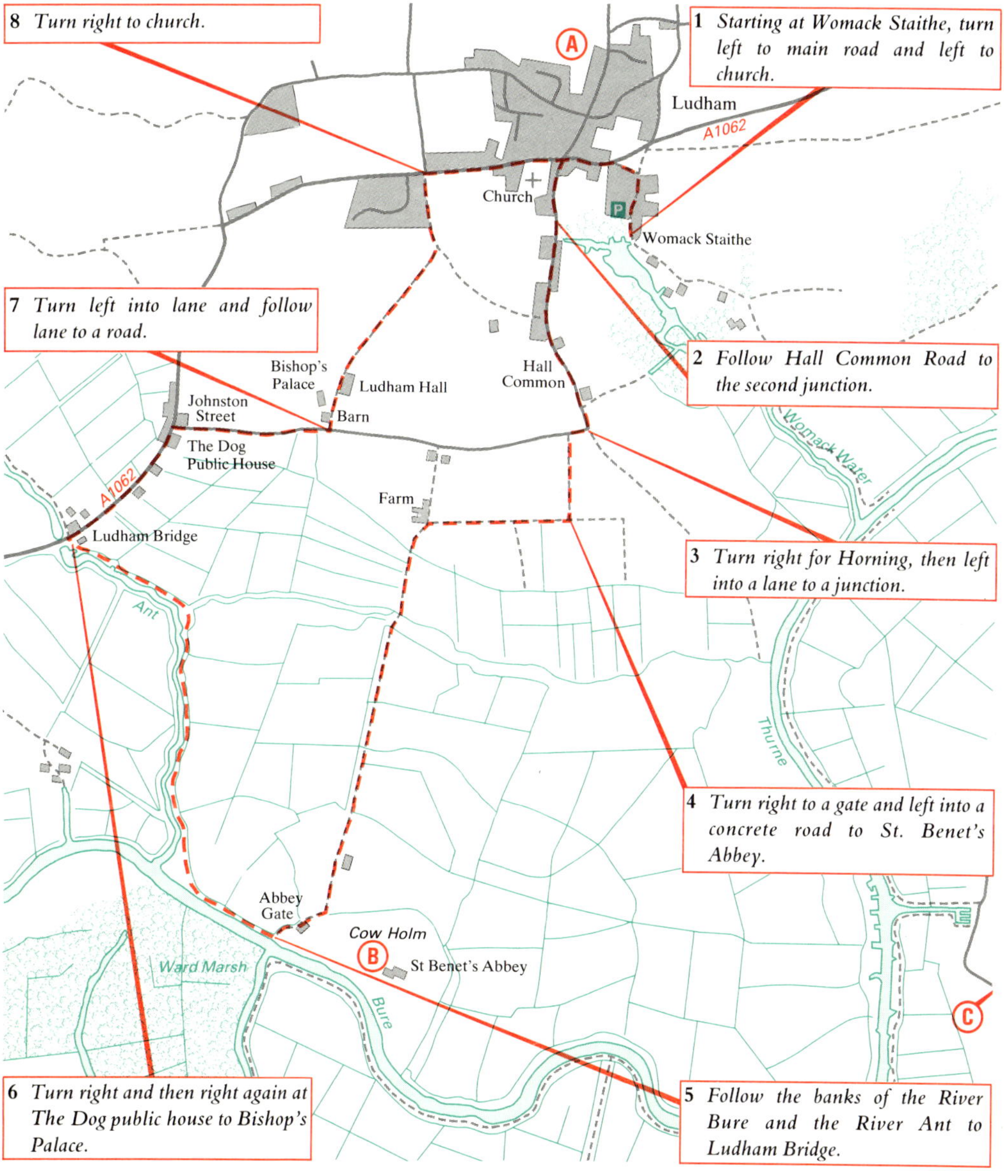

1 *Starting at Womack Staithe, turn left to main road and left to church.*

2 *Follow Hall Common Road to the second junction.*

3 *Turn right for Horning, then left into a lane to a junction.*

4 *Turn right to a gate and left into a concrete road to St. Benet's Abbey.*

5 *Follow the banks of the River Bure and the River Ant to Ludham Bridge.*

6 *Turn right and then right again at The Dog public house to Bishop's Palace.*

7 *Turn left into lane and follow lane to a road.*

8 *Turn right to church.*

Walk 8

SALHOUSE BROAD

4 miles (6.4km) Easy; shoes or boots

The walk can start from the car park or the moorings on the Broad at (1).

A Few Broads are more beautiful than the one in Salhouse. Sequestered by trees and reeds from the River Bure and reached by a sound footpath from the straggling village, it is certainly a favourite place. On its southern side, there is a firm strip where the fields slope down to the edge of the Broad so that a clear view opens across the water. The village takes its name from the sallows or pussy willows which are common on the damp ground near the Broad.

An important industry is the harvesting and sale of Norfolk reed to the building trade as a thatching material. Some concern, to put it mildly, was shown by Norfolk reed farmers in 1986 when a small item in the popular BBC programme 'The Archers' unfavourably compared Norfolk thatch with its Austrian competitors. Conservationists in a campaign against both the discharge of phosphate-rich effluent by the Water Authority and also the nitrates seeping into the Broad from surrounding farmland had said that it damaged and weakened the reed. Angry reed farmers dumped loads of their beloved reeds upon the doorstep of the Norwich BBC studios and caused 'The Archers' to hastily amend its view and declare the health of a thriving industry.

B Salhouse Church, with a sturdy tower at the end of a long thatched roof, stands near an Elizabethan Hall in a park. Firs and elms shade the churchyard and a great oak stands near the lych gate. A hedge of box and yew borders the church path to the south door, through which you see the 14th-century nave with carved capitals on its arcades except for one with eight little impish heads. Like many Norfolk churches, the original village, built of the reeds and mud (wattle and daub) which once surrounded it, has been abandoned and lost. In this village there was no disaster; increased trade and prosperity resulted in the construction of a new village but, in many cases, the old villages died through plague, pestilence or economic ruin.

Over

Walk 8
Salhouse Broad continued

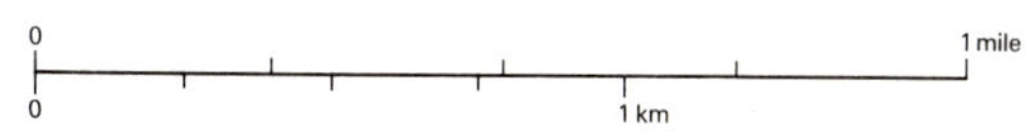

1 *From the car park, follow the path to Salhouse Broad. Then return to the road in which you turn right to a fork.*

2 *Take the Norwich road to the second junction and turn right into a drive past a white cottage.*

3 *Continue into a footpath and then walk along the field's left edge to a gap. Go through and left to the church.*

4 *Go ahead to a road and turn right but, at the end of the churchyard, turn left and continue straight over a field to Haggs Wood.*

5 *Follow the right edge to a corner then left, to wooden rails. Cross onto a path leading you to a railway.*

6 *Turn right in a track to a road.*

7 *Turn left under a bridge and then right into a farm track.*

8 *Follow this track to a cottage and turn right then left to a wood and right to a railway track.*

9 *Cross into a grassy lane and out to a road. Turn left to the hill bottom.*

10 *Turn right onto a track with a pond and a wood on your left. Follow the track to its end. Join another track. Turn right but when the track bends left into Hospital Farm, go ahead into a green lane.*

11 *Follow the lane to a road and turn left.*

12 *Just past a farm, turn right and up a bank to a stile. Cross and walk along the right edge of the field to another stile. Cross this and walk straight over the next field to a path on its far side.*

13 *Turn left and walk along right-hand field edges to a road.*

14 *Turn right to a pond and into Ranworth Road to a fork. The car park is straight ahead.*

Walk 9
LANGLEY ABBEY AND LANGLEY MARSH
4 miles (6.4km) Easy; strong shoes necessary, shorts unsuitable

The walk can start at The Wherry Inn at (1) or at moorings in Langley Dyke at (2). You will need permission from the publican to park at The Wherry Inn but cars may be parked safely on nearby road verges.

A An interesting feature of Broadland is the large number of monastic ruins dating from the late Saxon and Norman times. In 1066, there were 35 monastries in England but by 1100 this number had grown by a factor of five.

Due to its proximity to the Continent and the many rivers that gave easy access to its interior, many of these monastic buildings arose in Norfolk. There was an increase also in the number of nunneries.

Sometimes, all that remains is a small pile of stones on the wide flat land; at other times, there will be arches, gateways and pinnacles which add greatly to the Broadland scenery. Langley Abbey falls into the latter category.

By 1535, Henry VIII was desperately short of money. Extravagance and foreign wars had destroyed the fortune left to him by his father. There was no hope of raising money from the usual sources.

As 'Supreme Head of the Church', however, he was fully aware that new sources were ready to be tapped. Religious houses were endowed with large estates and enormous potential income. Did the monks really need so much money?

To be fair, the monasteries had, to some extent, outlived their useful functions by the 16th century. They were in need of some reform and stimulus. A new industrial age was in progress into which the decaying grandeur of the past could not be easily adapted.

The king's first step was to convince the public that the monasteries were not only redundant but also a scandal and that it would be a service to the community to abolish them. An Act of Parliament was duly drawn up and presented to the House, claiming that 'manifest sin, vicious, carnel and abominable living is daily committed in the small religious houses'.

A rapacious king and a subservient House thereby destroyed one of England's most ancient institutions. The monks had established the first schools, fed the poor, nursed the sick and provided hospitality to the traveller. In three years, monastic houses became quarries for farmers to build their barns and monastic lands were transferred to lay owners.

From the comfortable Wherry Inn, we can see the ruins of a rich abbey incorporated into a farm across the fields (private property). Across the road is the entrance to the head of Langley Dyke, specially dug to provide river access to the monastic buildings.

'The Wherry Inn' has been so named for at least 140 years and probably owes its origins to the busy early commercial usage of the dyke. Wherry men worked hard loading and unloading their cargoes which was thirsty work, and the Inn is a monument to those days of river transport.

This particular monument has been able to vigorously adapt to modern times with good food and drink for the holiday boats and fishermen who now throng the dyke and river during the holiday season.

B The Cantley sugar factory on the bank of the Yare is a downright ugly but, nevertheless, impressive sight. Built to service the many farms in the area and their annual crop of sugar beet, the clanking, steaming machines are continually adapting to the new industrial age.

Each year, with the beet harvest, lorries converge upon the plant over mud-strewn roads. This is part of the 'campaign', as it is called, to provide for the nation's sugar bowls. Many will say its product is useless and redundant but a larger number make eager use of all its sweetness.

Over

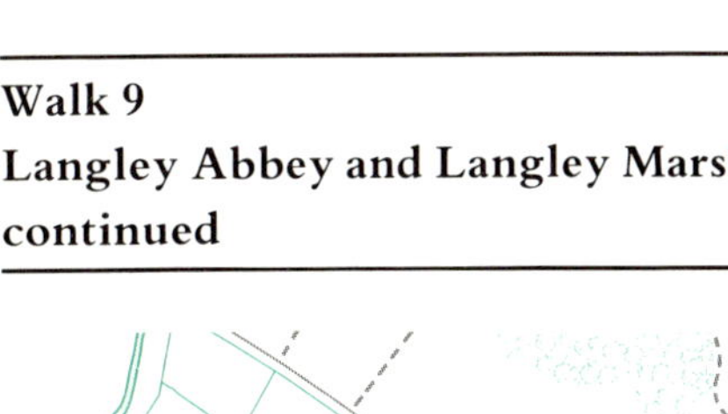

Walk 9
Langley Abbey and Langley Marsh continued

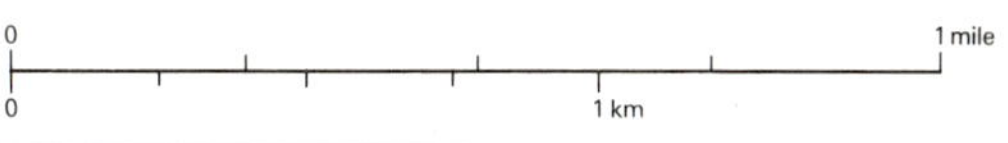

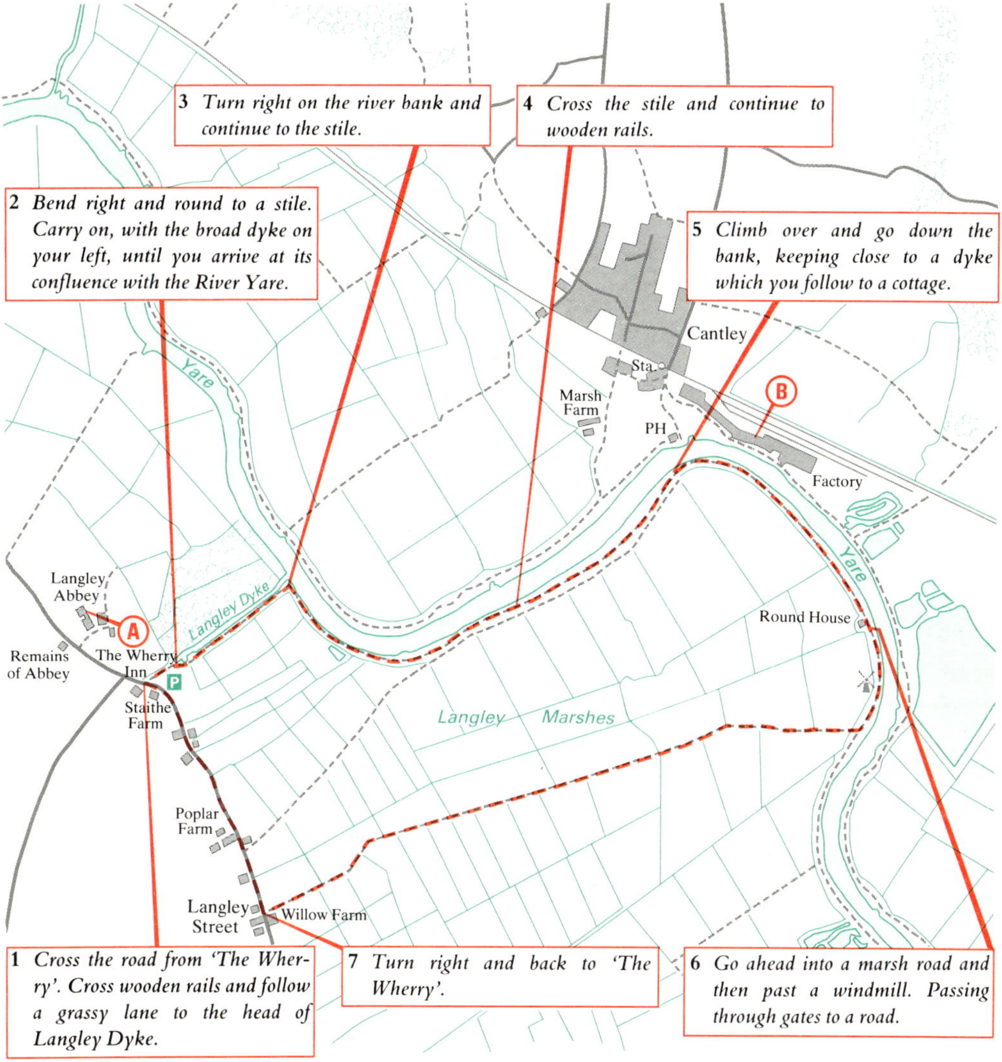

1. *Cross the road from 'The Wherry'. Cross wooden rails and follow a grassy lane to the head of Langley Dyke.*
2. *Bend right and round to a stile. Carry on, with the broad dyke on your left, until you arrive at its confluence with the River Yare.*
3. *Turn right on the river bank and continue to the stile.*
4. *Cross the stile and continue to wooden rails.*
5. *Climb over and go down the bank, keeping close to a dyke which you follow to a cottage.*
6. *Go ahead into a marsh road and then past a windmill. Passing through gates to a road.*
7. *Turn right and back to 'The Wherry'.*

Walk 10

FILBY TO RUNHAM

6 miles (9.7km) Moderate; good shoes required

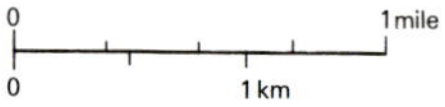

0 1 mile
0 1 km

Parking is unrestricted in the village at (1). Boat users may moor near the mill at (8).

A The brick towers of derelict windmills are a reminder of the strenuous efforts made in the 18th and 19th centuries to reclaim marshland and put it to good use. Local grains were ground into flour by mills on the higher ground of this wide and windy landscape.

The mill in Mautby is a post mill and rare in Norfolk. Its sails are made to face the wind by the full rotation of the mill on a central post. The more typical Norfolk mill has a rotating cap.

Mr and Mrs Prior spent three devoted years restoring this post mill which has added delightfully to this part of the Broadland landscape. They are always pleased to explain its works, controls and stability.

B The mill on the Runham marshes is a Norfolk windpump which is being renovated by a local farmer who is restoring a traditional feature to the Broadland landscape.

It is doubtful whether any existing mills were built before the 18th century. Their battered brick cones now stand oddly where they have been either abandoned for modern pumps or damaged by accident.

Most windmills had a small, vertical fan-tail in the side opposite the four main sails to keep them facing the wind. In earlier days, the sails were cloth-covered but movable wooden vanes or shutters were introduced in the 19th century. These could be opened or shut at will so that the mill could be started or stopped. A weight was also attached to the vanes to adjust them to the strength of the wind. Many an earlier mill was set on fire through driving too fast in a very high wind. Lightning, wind pressure and lop-sided subsidence also brought destruction.

The sails drove paddle wheels to lift the water from the mill sump where water flowed in from a thousand acres of marsh.

These things can now be seen in the restoration of the windpump as we pass closely to its site.

1 *Take a path on the left of the Fox and Hounds in Filby and follow it to a fork.*

2 *Go right, between a field and trees to another fork. Ignore right fork and go ahead to a field corner.*

3 *Go through into the next field and follow right edges to a road opposite a post mill.*

4 *Turn right for ½ mile (0.8km) to a junction signposted for Runham. Turn left to another junction.*

5 *Turn right for Runham to a junction by a kiosk and take the minor road past the village hall to the methodist church.*

6 *Turn left and soon right in a path past a paddock to a marsh road.*

7 *Follow the road to the River Bure. Turn left to Runham Mill, on the bank if it has been recently cut. Otherwise, keep to the marsh road.*

8 *Continue to a stile in a wire fence on the bank top.*

9 *Cross stile and walk along the bank top. Then turn left, down onto a track and turn left past a farm to a road. Turn left to another road on a corner.*

10 *Continue your direction to a crossroads. Go over into the road for Filby until you reach a junction.*

11 *Go ahead onto an unpaved lane to another junction (use field on right if lane is blocked).*

12 *Cross left to follow a field's right edge to a gap.*

13 *Pass through and ahead over fields to Filby Church.*

14 *Turn left through a gateway and along the churchyard wall to another gateway. Follow the path ahead to the Fox and Hounds.*

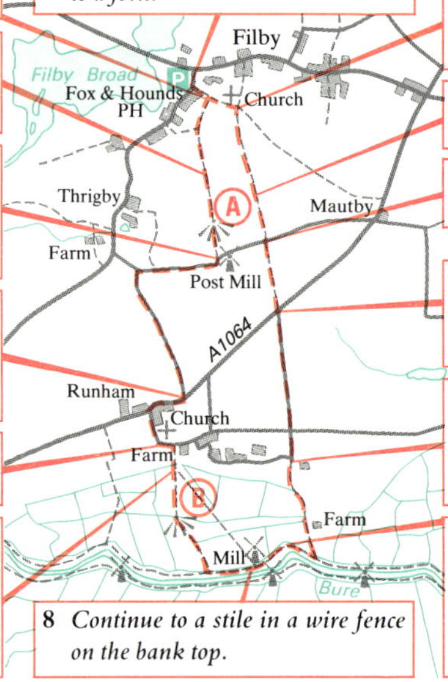

Walk 11

WHITLINGHAM COUNTRYSIDE

6 miles (9.7km) Moderate; strong shoes recommended

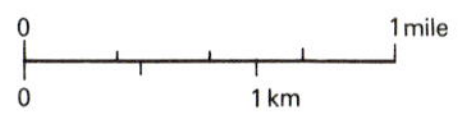

The walk can commence from the car park in Whitlingham Country Park or from boats at the riverside mooring.

A This picturesque area is now a country park set up by the local authority and substantially funded by the Countryside Commission. The park was used in the 1840s when the 'pleasure loving populace' of Norwich flocked to this attractive spot on daily excursions. Long before the days of motor cars or the power boat, people walked or rowed from Norwich to Whitlingham, which was one of a series of riverside beauty spots along the River Yare.

It was also a place of work: the steep hill behind the park is almost solid chalk, which was excavated during the last century to be burnt in local kilns for lime. At the river's edge, the white layers in the bank are where the chalk was piled ready for collection by wherry.

B The romantic ruin high on the edge of the hill overlooking the river is St. Andrew's Church, unused since 1630.

C The surrounding countryside was densely populated in prehistoric times by Stone Age man and a surprising collection of animals. In Norwich Castle Museum, which every visitor to Norwich should visit, a diorama of this area has been constructed with elephants, rhinos, wolves and tigers padding around. Flint weapons and tools have been found in great abundance.

1 *Leave Whitlingham Country Park and walk past a wood towards the works.*

2 *Turn left into a concrete road through the works. Ignore a sharp bend to the right and walk straight ahead into a track.*

3 *Just past an 'Entry Forbidden' notice, turn right into a field to follow an uncultivated strip uphill to a gate.*

4 *Pass through the gate and turn left into the track to its end in a lane.*

5 *Turn left for a quarter of a mile (0.4km) to turn right opposite a transformer, through a black iron gate.*

6 *Follow the track which bends left past a wall, then right, uphill past cottages into a lane.*

7 *Turn right to arrive at a junction by cottages. Turn right into a road.*

8 *Go downhill and just past Kirby House. Turn left through an iron gate into a field.*

9 *Cut a wide left corner to wooden rails about halfway along a hedge.*

10 *Cross and continue your direction over the next field to pass closely to the corner of a wood and straight to the far side.*

11 *Pass through a gap and turn left into a field corner. Turn right and continue along the left edge but when it bends sharply left, go diagonally left past a hollow to a gate and into a road.*

12 *Turn right for a short distance, then right again, into a concrete road back to the works and the Country Park.*

Walk 12

UPTON STAITHE TO ACLE

5 miles (8km) Moderate; strong shoes, shorts unsuitable

Parking available on Upton Staithe and mooring in Upton Dyke (1).

A The enclosure Acts of the 18th century made possible the construction of numerous boat dykes and landing staithes which were built close to villages and were usually given the nearest village's name. This improved trade between communities because transport was more readily available. Besides the import into the area of coal and timber by wherry, marl was conveyed for spreading upon the adjacent arable areas as fertiliser, while thatching reed and osiers for basket-making were a valuable export.

Now, of course, the straight dykes leading to the public staithes or landing places supply the needs of boats and hoiliday makers in their hundreds.

B The Domesday book records populous villages around Acle and many sheep. Daniel Defoe in his wanderings recorded in 1722 that lean cattle were brought in spring to marshes between Acle and Yarmouth where they fed voraciously on the lush grass and 'waxed monstrous fat'. Yet, by the close of the 18th century, we read accounts of journeys in which water reached as far as the knee joint of a horse. The ground was sinking and it became necessary to excavate more drains and dykes with banks and draining mills to reclaim the prosperity of the marsh. The process has continued until modern times but the change wrought upon the landscape has horrified conservationists. Until recently, great flocks of migratory birds came in the autumn but the drier marsh no longer attracts them. New legislation about to come into effect will restore this great area as a winter feeding ground for wide varieties of wild fowl and other birds.

C Acle has a market on Tuesdays and Thursdays. A few thatched houses and cottages look over its centre, which is busy with traffic. Near the Norwich end, a fine old church stands quietly at the end of an avenue of limes. Those who like to visit churches will no doubt make for this one which has something unique: on the chancel wall, a 15th-century rector has inscribed a prayer in Latin which warns the reader to pray and remember his sins.

Over

Walk 12
Upton Staithe to Acle continued

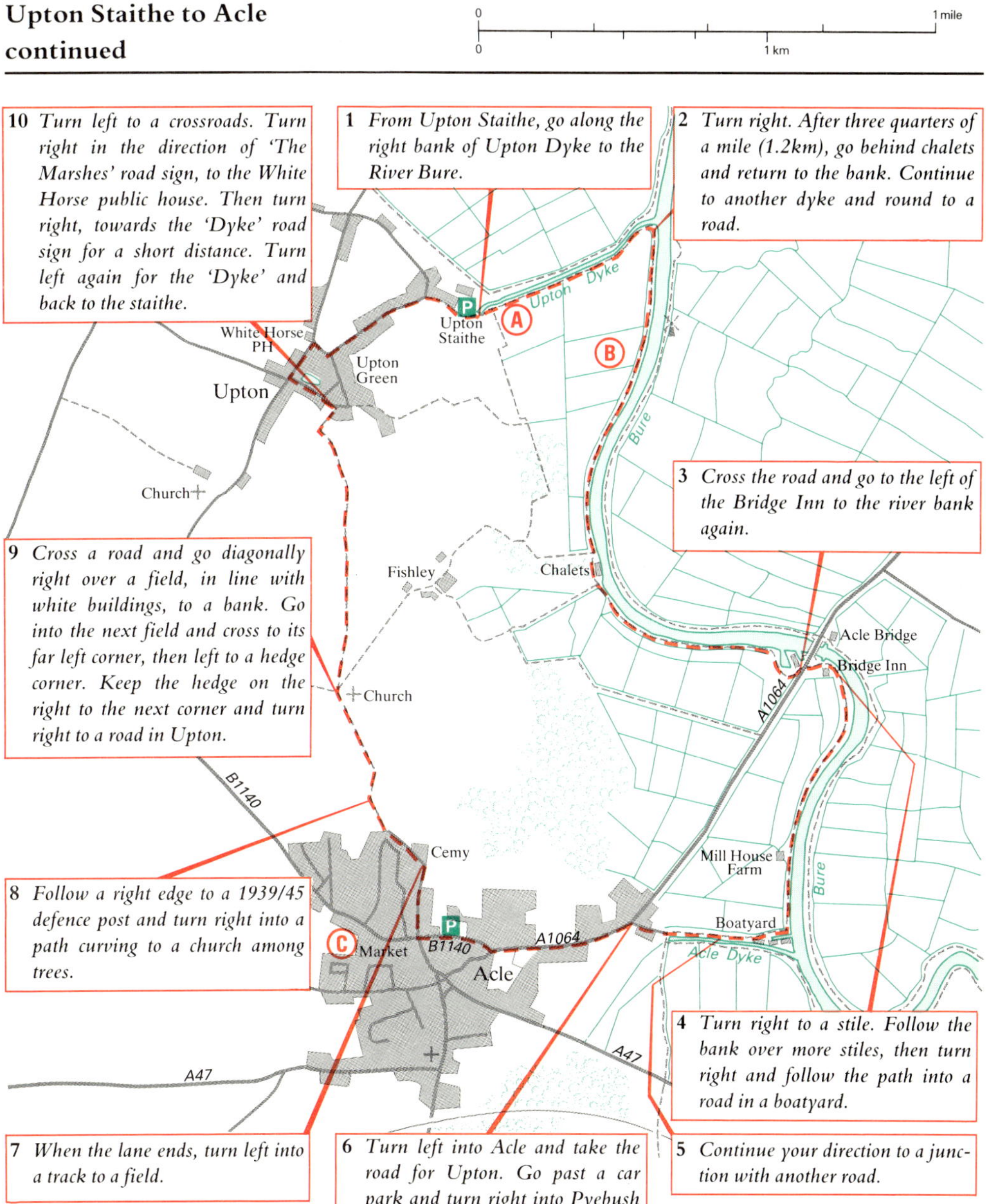

1 *From Upton Staithe, go along the right bank of Upton Dyke to the River Bure.*

2 *Turn right. After three quarters of a mile (1.2km), go behind chalets and return to the bank. Continue to another dyke and round to a road.*

3 *Cross the road and go to the left of the Bridge Inn to the river bank again.*

4 *Turn right to a stile. Follow the bank over more stiles, then turn right and follow the path into a road in a boatyard.*

5 *Continue your direction to a junction with another road.*

6 *Turn left into Acle and take the road for Upton. Go past a car park and turn right into Pyebush Lane.*

7 *When the lane ends, turn left into a track to a field.*

8 *Follow a right edge to a 1939/45 defence post and turn right into a path curving to a church among trees.*

9 *Cross a road and go diagonally right over a field, in line with white buildings, to a bank. Go into the next field and cross to its far left corner, then left to a hedge corner. Keep the hedge on the right to the next corner and turn right to a road in Upton.*

10 *Turn left to a crossroads. Turn right in the direction of 'The Marshes' road sign, to the White Horse public house. Then turn right, towards the 'Dyke' road sign for a short distance. Turn left again for the 'Dyke' and back to the staithe.*

Walk 13

POTTER HEIGHAM-THURNE-SHALLAM DYKE

6 miles (9.7km) Moderate; strong shoes or boots, shorts unsuitable

A Potter Heigham is a busy boat hire centre, always thronged with visitors in the summer. Since the 13th century, an old grey stone bridge has crossed the River Thurne. It has a low rounded middle arch and a pointed one on each side. Many an incautious holiday maker has found navigation through the arches in a tidal river to be a tricky matter, before sliding safely through into one of the finest stretches of Broadland.

B At the long curve of the river bank to the mill at Thurne, the landscape of windmills and sailing boats was beloved by Edwardian artists. Although the rich meadows that lined the banks in those days have been drained to make arable fields, there remain flowers, plants and wild growth upon our path. The windmill at the end of Thurne Dyke has been carefully restored by the Norfolk Windmills Trust and is open to the public. The fantail that keeps the rotating head and sails facing into the wind and the slats which controlled the rotation of the sails can all be clearly seen. The long dyke and village staithe are also good examples of the way of life and trade in Broadland in times past when so much depended upon water traffic.

C Shallam Dyke is a lush example of the progressive stage in Broadland when swamp carr is changing into alder carr. Butterflies feed upon marsh thistles and the swampier parts are a mass of colour in the midsummer. The more progressive stage which borders the dyke is a cool green mass of alder and willow growing completely wild. Alder wood stands a great deal of soaking and drying and was an excellent choice as material for the construction of lock gates for canals. The only Norfolk examples are those on the North Walsham and Dilham canal, the locks of which have been abandoned for many years but can still, occasionally, be seen holding back the waters. Walk 14 to Tonnage Bridge crosses one of the derelict locks.

Over

Walk 13
Potter Heigham – Thurne – Shallam Dyke continued

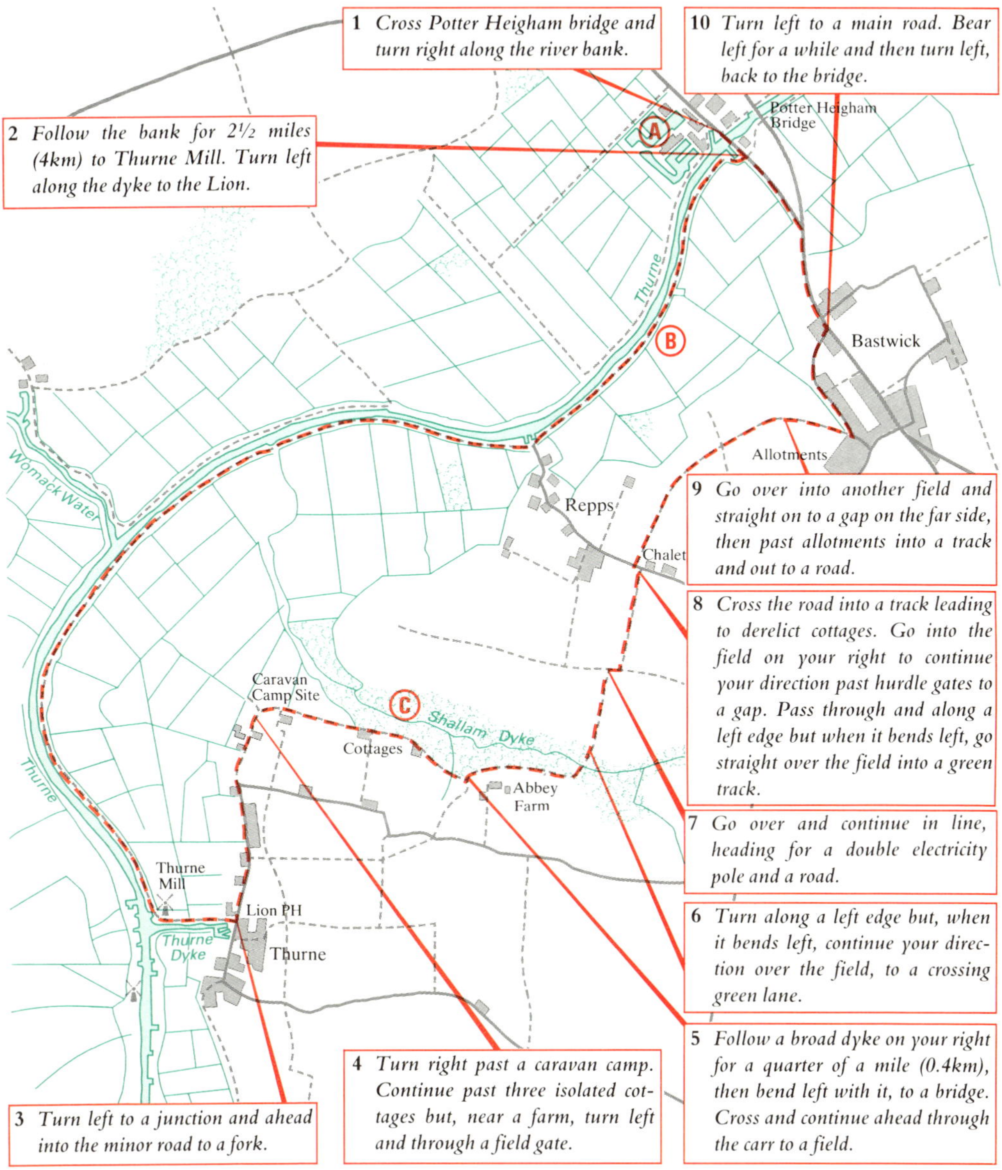

1 *Cross Potter Heigham bridge and turn right along the river bank.*

2 *Follow the bank for 2½ miles (4km) to Thurne Mill. Turn left along the dyke to the Lion.*

3 *Turn left to a junction and ahead into the minor road to a fork.*

4 *Turn right past a caravan camp. Continue past three isolated cottages but, near a farm, turn left and through a field gate.*

5 *Follow a broad dyke on your right for a quarter of a mile (0.4km), then bend left with it, to a bridge. Cross and continue ahead through the carr to a field.*

6 *Turn along a left edge but, when it bends left, continue your direction over the field, to a crossing green lane.*

7 *Go over and continue in line, heading for a double electricity pole and a road.*

8 *Cross the road into a track leading to derelict cottages. Go into the field on your right to continue your direction past hurdle gates to a gap. Pass through and along a left edge but when it bends left, go straight over the field into a green track.*

9 *Go over into another field and straight on to a gap on the far side, then past allotments into a track and out to a road.*

10 *Turn left to a main road. Bear left for a while and then turn left, back to the bridge.*

Walk 14

DILHAM-TONNAGE BRIDGE

6 miles (9.7km) Moderate; good shoes, shorts unsuitable

Parking in Dilham or at the Cross Keys by permission of the landlord (1). Moorings available in Dilham Cut (2).

This walk may be started at the Cross Keys or on Dilham Staithe. Before starting the walk, a visit to the Norfolk Wildfowl Conservation Centre attached to the Cross Keys will improve your enjoyment of this and many other walks in Broadland.

A Dilham Staithe was the navigable limit of the River Ant until the North Walsham and Dilham Canal was completed around the year 1826. Before that time, goods being transported by boat from Yarmouth to North Walsham were unloaded on the staithe and taken the rest of the way by cart. A turnpike road existed but, like all monopolies, the company that owned it made very high charges. A company was, therefore, formed to build and operate a canal using the experience and skills gained by the 'navigators' during the 18th-century canal building boom. Unfortunately, it relied for its head of water on the Antingham Ponds which proved, in practice, to be insufficient to fill the locks more than three times a day. The canal was, therefore, only a limited success but it continued in use until the 1930s.

B Tonnage Bridge was, presumably, the point where the cargo weights were checked and the tolls were taken. In 1837, these varied between 3d and 5d a ton for coal but more was charged for wine on the principle that those who could afford wine could also afford higher taxes. The bridge has recently been rebuilt and widened after damage was caused by heavy modern farm machinery but a serious attempt has been made at restoration to its earlier appearance by using the original bricks.

As so often in Broadland, great pleasure can be derived from letting the imagination run. We can see the 12 ton wherries sailing on these slow waters: a friendly wind and the watchful skill of a skipper handling the boat smoothly to Honing Lock 1½ miles (2.4km) away. A day in the doldrums and we can feel for the sweating crewman 'man-hauling' the wherry on this lovely route through meadows because no tow path was ever constructed.

C After crossing the Honing Lock, a path leads to a disused railway line, now a recreational path imaginatively named 'Weavers Way'. The weaving trade was established in Norfolk in the 16th century by encouraging the immigration of Flemish weavers into this great area of countless flocks of sheep. Nearby is the village of Worstead, which gave its name to a newly devised weave. Its great church demonstrates the enormous wealth of the 16th century and is well worth a visit if you have the time.

Over

Walk 14
Dilham – Tonnage Bridge continued

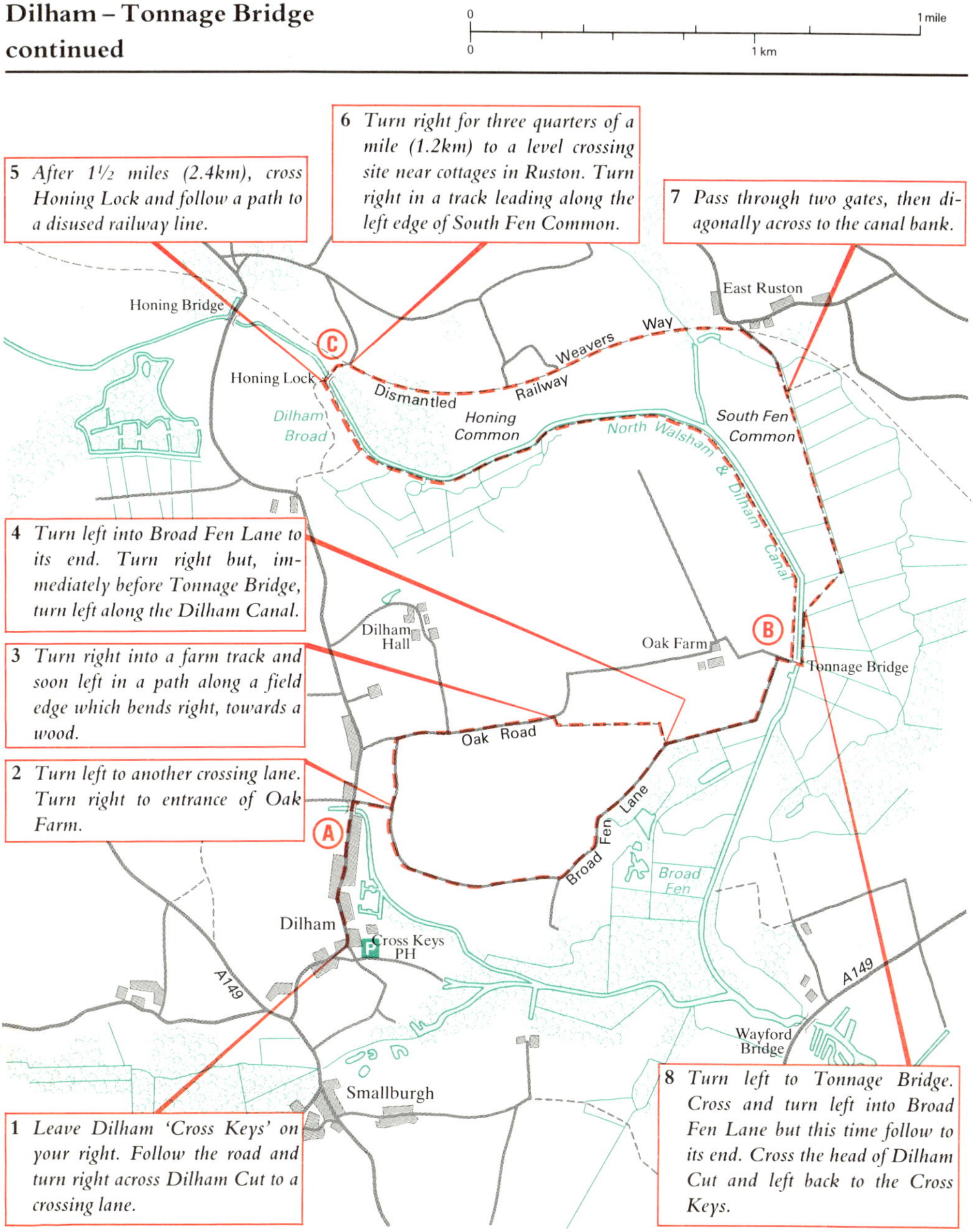

1 *Leave Dilham 'Cross Keys' on your right. Follow the road and turn right across Dilham Cut to a crossing lane.*

2 *Turn left to another crossing lane. Turn right to entrance of Oak Farm.*

3 *Turn right into a farm track and soon left in a path along a field edge which bends right, towards a wood.*

4 *Turn left into Broad Fen Lane to its end. Turn right but, immediately before Tonnage Bridge, turn left along the Dilham Canal.*

5 *After 1½ miles (2.4km), cross Honing Lock and follow a path to a disused railway line.*

6 *Turn right for three quarters of a mile (1.2km) to a level crossing site near cottages in Ruston. Turn right in a track leading along the left edge of South Fen Common.*

7 *Pass through two gates, then diagonally across to the canal bank.*

8 *Turn left to Tonnage Bridge. Cross and turn left into Broad Fen Lane but this time follow to its end. Cross the head of Dilham Cut and left back to the Cross Keys.*

Walk 15

WAVENEY VALLEY

10 miles (16km) Easy but parts of Breydon Bank have undergrowth in summer, shorts unsuitable

This walk commences in Great Yarmouth and ends in Haddiscoe. Trains run fairly frequently between Haddiscoe, Yarmouth and Norwich. There are moorings in Haddiscoe enabling some crew members to enjoy this walk while others sail the craft leisurely to Haddiscoe to meet them at the end of the day.

A Breydon Water is a large salt water lake about 4 miles (6.4km) long. At its widest, it measures about three quarters of a mile (1.2km). At full tide in summer, it is a glittering sheet of water dotted with boats and a few large pleasure craft gliding musically along. In the autumn, flocks of migrating birds feed upon its wide mud flats as the tide recedes. Out in the channel, you will probably see black cormorants and white gulls.

Almost every type of duck and goose has been sighted on Breydon. Grebes, curlews, herons and the occasional kingfisher feed on the numerous small fish. Widgeon, shovelers, godwits, shelducks and spoonbills will be seen busily picking crustaceans and insects along its wide banks.

This waterway was used in the middle ages for transporting wool to Yarmouth for European trade. The great prosperity which this brought over several centuries can still be seen in the sometimes quite magnificent village churches throughout the county.

B Burgh Castle is probably the largest Roman fort in Britain and its 15ft (4.6m) high walls are a most impressive sight from the lane near Burgh Church. The castle is in the care of the government who have placed an interpretative board at the entrance outlining its history.

From this vantage point, we have a splendid view of Broadland; rivers, sailing boats, windmills, marshes, cattle and reedbeds. This is the landscape which the government hopes to preserve as an Environmentally Sensitive Area. The danger, at one time, was excessive drainage and a conversion to more profitable cereal growing. With the co-operation of its owners, this fine panorama will now be saved for succeeding generations.

C Fritton Church is one of the gems of East Anglia. The Reverend Wilkinson, in a history available in the church, points out its Saxon architectural features. To the layman, its charm is immediate, both within its small interior and from the outside where its isolated setting lends character to the round tower, thatched nave and rounded apse.

D The New Cut was proposed in 1814 when there was a strong rivalry between Yarmouth and Norwich. In order to avoid unloading goods in Yarmouth Quay and then reloading them into wherries which carried them inland, Norwich wanted to dredge the Yare so that sea-going ships could reach the city. The workers at Yarmouth fought to keep their profitable position as middlemen but they lost the argument and the New Cut, when completed in 1832, by-passed Yarmouth and connected the Yare via the Waveney into Lowestoft. As a result, shipping was able to reach Norwich directly from the sea. The New Cut's 2 mile (3.2km) length can be seen from the Haddiscoe Bridge. The importance of the Cut was greatly reduced by the advent of railways and Yarmouth regained its prosperity.

Over

Walk 15
Waveney Valley continued

1 *Cross Southtown Bridge in the direction of Lowestoft. After a short distance, turn right into Steam Mill Lane and, when it bends left, follow a short path ahead into Crittens Lane. After a few yards, turn left past a playground to crossroads. Turn right to the end of the road and into a rough track to a new bridge.*

2 *Pass under and along the edge of Breydon Water to a gate. Go through and, after a quarter of a mile (0.4km), keep close to piling and continue on a bank to a stile.*

3 *Follow the bank top until the piling bends sharply right. Continue your direction, down the bank, over the meadows, heading for Berney Mill in the distance. You will come to a stile on the far bank.*

4 *Turn left to the end of the bank, then uphill to Burgh Church. Take a path on its left to the Roman Fort.*

5 *Go into the fort and down steps to the river bank. Turn left to the Fisherman's Bar.*

6 *Turn left uphill and turn right in a footpath past a harbour and back to the river bank. After a short way, turn left to a stile and into a green lane.*

7 *Follow the lane to another stile and into a lane which bends left into a rough walk to a road on a corner in Belton.*

8 *Turn right for three quarters of a mile (1.2km) to 'The Tavern'. Turn right in Sandy Lane.*

9 *Follow the lane which bends right and becomes truly sandy. After three quarters of a mile (1.2km), you pass beneath the second set of power lines and shortly after passing a cottage, turn left in a closely mown path on the left of the next cottage.*

10 *Follow the path, which becomes rough, straight over a field to a hedge. Follow the right edge to a gap, then the left edge of another field into a short track and out to the A143*

11 *Turn right for a short distance and left through a kissing gate, then straight to Fritton Church.*

12 *Turn right, into a sunken lane and rejoin the A143. Follow for a mile (1.6km) to Haddiscoe bridge, under which runs the New Cut.*

13 *Cross the bridge and turn left for half a mile (0.8km) to Haddiscoe Station.*

Walk 16

HICKLING GREEN

3 miles (4.8km) Easy

This walk can commence from the car park (1) or from the 'Pleasure Boat' Inn (2).

A Walk 4 follows the southern edge of Hickling Broad and its great ronds of reed and sedge. By contrast, we can see, on this walk, the full expanse of the largest Broad in Norfolk: 400 acres (162 hectares) of surface spread before us. The company, too, is different. On the southern side, there is the rustle of reeds and bird song and an occassional stroller. On the northern side, during the summer, the old fashioned Pleasure Boat Inn will be filled with holiday makers in its low raftered bar.

Nevertheless, only a short stroll from the moorings and the dinghy parks, you will find yourself walking through quiet country lanes and farmland into a pleasant village. If you have time to spare, go to the Warden's Office marked on the map. There are five nature trails starting from the office, where you can obtain leaflets and descriptions to help widen your accumulating knowledge of this marvellous area of England.

1 *Leave the car park in Hickling Green. Turn left past the church. Use path behind bank at roadside, to a junction signposted for 'Hickling Broad'.*

2 *Turn left for a quarter of a mile (0.4km) and then go past the 'Pleasure Boat' public house to the edge of the Broad where you can admire the view.*

3 *Return to road. Turn right and pass a dinghy park and then reed beds, until you reach an unpaved road on your right.*

4 *Turn right, along the edge of the Broad and into a lane leading to a farm.*

5 *Turn left through the farm and follow a concrete road to a lane.*

6 *Turn left for half a mile (0.8km). Ignore first right turn and continue to a road junction.*

7 *Turn right through the village to the 'Greyhound' public house. Turn left to car park.*

Church
Town Street
Hickling Green
Greyhound PH
Church
P
Hickling
The Causeway
Stubb
Hickling Heath
Hill Common
Staithe Road
A
Pleasure Boat PH
Manor Farm
Willow Farm
Stubb Road
Heath Road
Hickling Broad
Warden's House

Walk 17

LODDON AND THE HARDLEY FLOOD

5 miles (8km) Easy; good boots or wellies essential

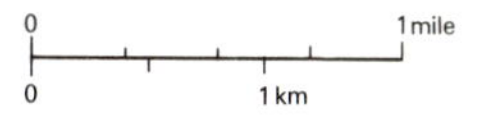

This walk can be started from Chedgrave Church where there are a few parking places. Otherwise, cars may be parked quite safely in the surrounding roads. Boat users may start at the moorings near Chedgrave Common or from the boatyard in Loddon.

Visitors to Loddon should take the opportunity to see its church of striking proportions and rare treasures.

A The Hardley Flood has the distinction, like Horsey Mere (Walk 28), of not being a true Broad in the sense that its origin was not in the peat digging of the Middle Ages. Most Broads were a consequence of the extraction of millions of cubic yards of peat for fuel by the peasants of this chilly county. Water then flowed in, the reeds grew, birds colonised the area and Broadland became an 'Area of Outstanding Natural Beauty'.

Hardley Flood is on low lying land that became a spillway for the river Chet. There are breaches in the river wall and the tidal water moves in freely. At high tides, there are a few wet patches and good footwear is needed at these times. That condition aside, the edge of the Flood is a place of particular beauty.

In the autumn, the winter wildfowl come wheeling in; teal, shoveller and shelduck. In the spring, the passing migrants include osprey, spoonbill and black tern. The mud fringes of the Flood attract waders, including the oyster catcher.

Pochard, tufted duck, gadwall and shoveller breed upon the Flood among a thriving colony of common terns. Hen harriers hunt across it and, occasionally, a bearded tit may be seen.

The Norfolk Naturalists Trust administers the 90 acres (36 hectares) of the Flood and provides hides for the keen bird watcher. Their office in The Close, Norwich, will supply the details.

B Hardley Hall, which you pass on the way back from the Flood, is a handsome Georgian house. The long track also provides a fine view over the water.

1 *From Chedgrave Church, cross a playground into a dell to a road. Turn right and, when the road bends right, go ahead over a stile to the River Chet.*

2 *Turn left on the bank to another stile. Cross and continue to the moorings. Continue to a footbridge. Cross and walk on to the next footbridge. The path may be wet at high tides as you go to a third footbridge.*

3 *Cross and continue to the head of the Flood. Turn left a few yards to turn right and follow the river to a stile.*

4 *Climb over and turn left to a crossroads near cottages. Go straight over and follow a track to a road.*

5 *Turn left back to Chedgrave Church and Loddon.*

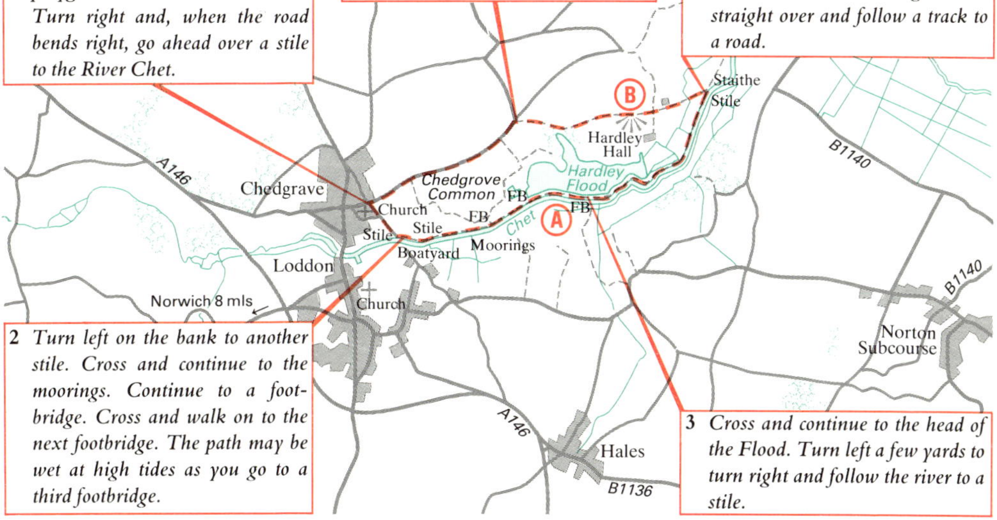

Walk 18

BARTON STAITHE TO BARTON TURF CHURCH 3 miles (4.8km) Easy

This walk starts on Barton Staithe where there is a car park and mooring for boats (**1**).

A boardwalk around Paddy's Dyke makes it possible to walk along the edge of the River Ant and through the alder carr but, in order to return to the car park, you must retrace the same route.

A The purpose of these 3 miles (4.8km) is not the flora and fauna of the Broads but to walk across the fields to one of those isolated churches which make Norfolk such an interesting and attractive county: The visitor pushes open the door of a country church and is often confronted by some masterpiece of mediaeval craftsmanship. Barton Turf is a good example.

The screen is the glory of the church. The parclose screens which crossed the aisles have been destroyed but the panels in the screen across the chancel arch are the finest in the county. William H. Hall gave his opinion that the beauty and deep spirituality displayed in the faces of its figures was the work of a qualified artist from the Abbey of St. Benet's (Walk 7).

The south screen was preserved from destruction by zealous 17th-century puritans because it was hidden behind a high backed pew. Among its figures is a rare portrait of Henry VI which is of great historical importance in the completion of the series of portraits of the Kings of England.

The great tower and the splendid perpendicular windows, built in 1400, are reminders of the enormous wealth of Norfolk in those days, based upon wool. Trade was assisted by the large number of rivers which provided an easy transport system in that era of poor roads. Prosperity in those days can still be gauged from the beauty and workmanship of churches like Barton Turf.

1 *From the car park on Barton Staithe, follow the road past Bittern Crescent to the next junction on the right. Turn right, past a hollow, to where another road comes in on the left.*

2 *Continue your direction, past a lane, then a methodist church, to Point Cottage in Pennygate. Turn left in the path into a field. Go along the left edge but when it bends sharply left, go straight ahead to a gap in the far hedge and into a road.*

3 *Turn right after a few yards, then left into a path slanting through a wood into a huge field. Cross in line with Barton Church and, when pylons appear, use them as a guide to the far hedge. Pass through, continue in line with the pylons, then to a gap opposite farm buildings into a road.*

4 *Turn left past Barton Church to a junction. Turn left for Barton Turf to another junction. Go ahead for Pennygate to a fork and then right, signposted for 'the river', to Barton Staithe.*

Walk 19

IRSTEAD SHOALS AND ALDERFEN BROAD

4 miles (6.4km) Moderate; strong shoes or boots recommended, shorts unsuitable

There is a car park at Irstead Shoals Staithe and mooring for a few boats. These four miles are an adventure for those who like to explore Norfolk's most secret places.

A There is a public footpath through the marsh and alder carr on the edge of Alderfen Broad where birds, frogs and a few grass snakes thrive. This is one of the few water spaces in Broadland still supporting white and yellow waterlilies upon its surface.

The Broad is an interesting example of the natural succession as shallow water is infilled by plants and colonised by swamp species into reed bed. The invasion of woody species brings the final stage in alder carr and the appearance of oak trees.

Irstead Church has distinctive oak seats which are 400 years old and are carved with dogs on the bench ends. It is an interesting and isolated place.

1 *From Irstead Shoals Staithe, follow the road to a junction. Continue to the next junction and turn left.*

2 *After a quarter of a mile (0.4km), opposite a thatched farm, turn right and go a short way ahead into a green lane. Follow the lane to its end, into a road. Turn left and join another road near bungalows. Go right, then round a right curve but, when the road curves left, cross white rails into woodland carr by a sluice.*

3 *Go straight ahead following yellow waymarks to an earthen bridge over a ditch. Cross and turn left. Keep the ditch on your left through undergrowth until the path becomes clearer and meets a crossing path. Turn right and straight to a staithe.*

4 *Turn left and walk approximately 100yds (91m) before turning right into a farm track. Follow the left edge of two fields into a corner and turn left through a gap.*

5 *Follow the right edge of a field and, shortly before a cottage, turn right, through a hedge and over a ditch, into a field. Go straight ahead and bend left at the end to iron rails on your right. Cross into a path and follow to a road.*

6 *Turn right and, when the lane ends at a cottage, go into the field on your left. Follow a right edge and, when it bends sharply right, turn left to walk over the field to a gap and onto a road.*

7 *Turn right and walk back to Irstead Shoals Staithe.*

Walk 20

CANTLEY

0 1 mile
0 1 km

7 miles (11.3km) or 2-mile (3.2km) short cut. Easy; strong shoes recommended. Short cut: leave walk at Malthouse Lane (4). Turn right to Cantley station.

This walk may be started from Cantley Station. Permission is needed to park at the Red House public house (1) but safe parking may be found at the roadside in Cantley. Moorings for boats in plenty (1).

A The banks of the River Yare have been heightened since the 18th century when windmills were introduced in 1750 and drainage improved. Between the protective bank and river, there are, in places, broad flats called ronds which have become colonised by reed beds, sedge and reed mace. In summer, there are colourful stretches of yellow iris, rosebay and dogrose.

B In the marshes on either side of this wide valley, there are long drainage ditches or dykes. When the water is clear and without excessive algae stimulated by nitrates from fertilisers, flowering rush, water soldier and frogbit appear. With new agreements made between the Broads Authority and the landowners, the marshes will be farmed in the traditional way and we shall see lilies again, amid the deep green pondweed and the rare marsh mallow.

Black cormorants on this walk perch in trees on the river bank. Groups of swans glide along the river in virgin white. Mallard ducks swim hungrily around the moored boats and a tense peregrine will quarter the marshes watching for mice.

Sails and motor boats complete the Norfolk scene beneath wide skies.

1 *From the 'Red House' Inn, follow the right bank of the river to a brick pump house.*

2 *Cross a fence and continue on the bank round a curve. Shortly after passing a power line, turn right, down the bank to an iron gate.*

3 *Follow a straight track to a fork and go left to a level crossing.*

4 *Go over and follow a lane ahead to Malthouse Lane. Cross the lane into a footpath opposite.*

5 *Go uphill to a house with a high wall. Turn left and follow a winding track round a sloping field to a road on the corner.*

6 *Turn right to a crossroads and go ahead in the direction of Freethorpe until you reach a junction.*

7 *Follow road for Freethorpe but, on a sharp left bend, go ahead down a bank to an overgrown iron hurdle.*

8 *Cross the fence into a field. Go ahead to the next fence. Cross into another field and ahead, passing to the left of a church before arriving at a road.*

9 *Turn right to a junction. Take road for Limpenhoe which leads to a fork. Continue for Limpenhoe and, on a sharp left bend, go ahead into an unpaved lane.*

10 *Continue into a green lane. Follow to a gate and into a rough road.*

11 *Turn right for a short way and then right through a wide gap in a hedge. Follow a faint track to a footbridge. Cross and turn right between a ditch and a high bank and walk for half a mile (0.8km) through high growth, at times, to join a factory road.*

12 *Follow road round bend and ahead into a green lane. Continue to an avenue and walk past houses to a road.*

13 *Turn left to a level crossing. Go over and take lane signposted for 'Red House' Inn.*

Walk 21

YARMOUTH AND MAUTBY

0 1 mile
0 1 km

6 miles (9.7km) Moderate with rough banks in places; strong shoes recommended, shorts unsuitable

Cars can be parked unrestrictedly in the vicinity of the Bure Hotel (1). There is a mooring for boats along the Yare nearby.

River banks are excellent places for bird watchers: we can watch as we walk, using the naked eye or, perhaps, a small pair of binoculars.

The experienced countrygoer will learn to name a bird by its flight as well as by its song. The swoop of a swallow in obvious contrast to the awkward flight of a crow is an extreme example but each bird has its ways which we learn to recognise at a glance.

In the Norfolk dialect, a heron is a harnser which makes sense of Hamlet's phrase 'I know a hawk from a handsaw'. As we compare the tense grace of a hawk over the marsh with the ungainly flight of a heron, the meaning of the phrase becomes clear.

A A mile of this walk passes through saltings near Three Mile House where terns, reed buntings and many wildfowl will be your companions. Listen for the reed bunting: its normal sound is a metallic 'chink' which changes in alarm, as you approach, to a 'chit' repeated many times. When it sings, while hanging from a reed stem, its song begins slowly with several 'tseek-tseek', then ends hurriedly with a sibilant 'tissis-sisk'.

Watch quietly and distinguish the male, with the black head and a white collar round his throat, from the brown headed female with pale buff eyebrows, a conspicuous black and white moustache and black streaks upon its breast.

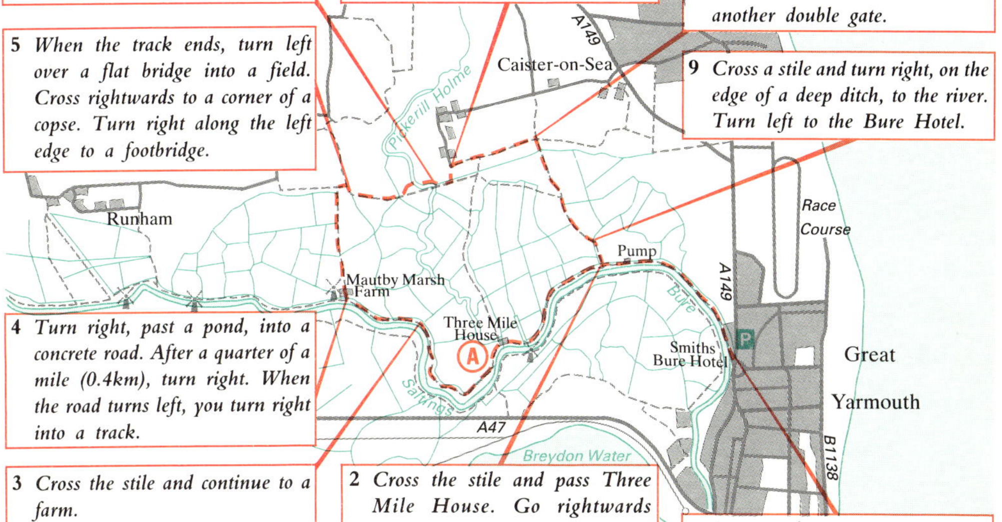

1 *Start at the Bure Hotel on the A149. Go to river bank and turn right for a mile (1.6km) to a stile.*

2 *Cross the stile and pass Three Mile House. Go rightwards round an inlet to another stile. Cross and follow a curve past saltings to another stile.*

3 *Cross the stile and continue to a farm.*

4 *Turn right, past a pond, into a concrete road. After a quarter of a mile (0.4km), turn right. When the road turns left, you turn right into a track.*

5 *When the track ends, turn left over a flat bridge into a field. Cross rightwards to a corner of a copse. Turn right along the left edge to a footbridge.*

6 *Cross and follow a ditch to a gate. Pass through into a track and continue to another track on a corner.*

7 *Turn right for a quarter of a mile (0.4km) and, when a road appears on your left, turn right in an unpaved road.*

8 *Follow to double gates and through into a concrete road. Continue through more gates and, when concrete ends, continue to another double gate.*

9 *Cross a stile and turn right, on the edge of a deep ditch, to the river. Turn left to the Bure Hotel.*

A149
Caister-on-Sea
Pickerill Holme
Runham
Mautby Marsh Farm
Three Mile House
Pump
Bure
Race Course
A149
Smiths Bure Hotel
P
Great Yarmouth
Saltings
A47
Breydon Water
B1138

Walk 22

BRAMERTON WOODS END

2 miles (3.2km) or 6 miles (9.7km) Easy; strong shoes recommended, shorts unsuitable

There is car parking on Bramerton Common (1) and moorings by the river bank (1).

The Bramerton Woods End Inn was one of the many places along the Yare which once had a ferry. In the days when almost all transport was by horse or by foot, a ferry boat was quite necessary to the prosperity of an Inn.

A The Woods End, moreover, was always known as a beauty spot by the people of Norwich. They loved to walk its paths and lanes and climb its gentle hills. Many would arrive on the Whitlingham side and expect a ferry to the Inn. Some would come by the pleasure boats which made excursions from Norwich on summer days.

The two mile walk described on the map was a popular Sunday stroll.

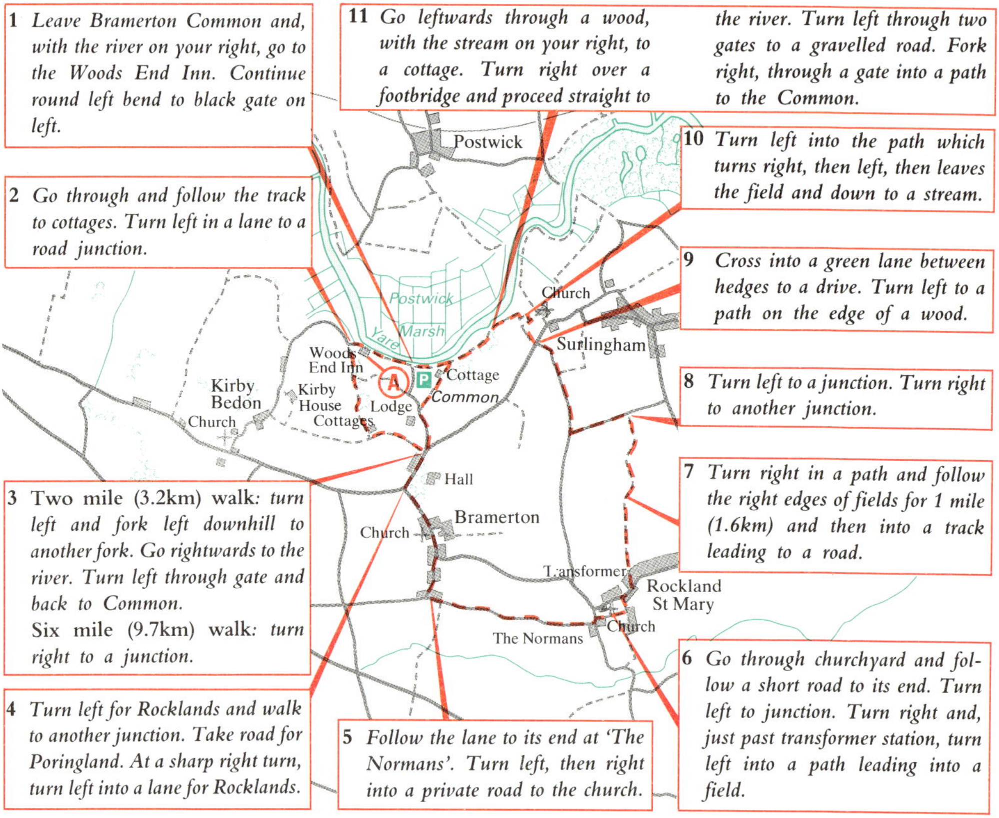

1 *Leave Bramerton Common and, with the river on your right, go to the Woods End Inn. Continue round left bend to black gate on left.*

2 *Go through and follow the track to cottages. Turn left in a lane to a road junction.*

3 Two mile (3.2km) walk: *turn left and fork left downhill to another fork. Go rightwards to the river. Turn left through gate and back to Common.*

Six mile (9.7km) walk: *turn right to a junction.*

4 *Turn left for Rocklands and walk to another junction. Take road for Poringland. At a sharp right turn, turn left into a lane for Rocklands.*

5 *Follow the lane to its end at 'The Normans'. Turn left, then right into a private road to the church.*

6 *Go through churchyard and follow a short road to its end. Turn left to junction. Turn right and, just past transformer station, turn left into a path leading into a field.*

7 *Turn right in a path and follow the right edges of fields for 1 mile (1.6km) and then into a track leading to a road.*

8 *Turn left to a junction. Turn right to another junction.*

9 *Cross into a green lane between hedges to a drive. Turn left to a path on the edge of a wood.*

10 *Turn left into the path which turns right, then left, then leaves the field and down to a stream.*

11 *Go leftwards through a wood, with the stream on your right, to a cottage. Turn right over a footbridge and proceed straight to the river. Turn left through two gates to a gravelled road. Fork right, through a gate into a path to the Common.*

Walk 23
SOUTH WALSHAM BROAD AND UPTON FEN

6 miles (9.7km) or 2 miles (3.2km) for those who want to spend time in the Nature Reserve. Easy; good shoes recommended

The walk starts at the car park near South Walsham Broad (1) or at the moorings (1).

We pass through a part of Upton Fen on this walk but the main entrance to the nature trail is at point X on the map between Fen House and Fen Cottage. The trail is open throughout the year. In addition to its colourful reed beds, its sedge beds contain bog myrtle and creeping willow. There are many types of orchid, including the marsh helleborine and the lesser butterfly orchid.

A colony of swallowtail butterflies are established and an exceptional quantity of dragonfly species including the rare Norfolk aeshna. White admirals and the comma butterfly are also numerous. The area is under the control of the Norfolk Naturalists Trust with offices at 72, The Close, Norwich.

A South Walsham Broad, at the beginning of the walk, is one of the most enchanting in Broadland. Almost surrounded by trees and reedbeds, it has one good staithe, where a full sight of its beauty can be gauged. The reedbeds in summer are bright with loosestrife, rosebay and the ubiquitous hemp agrimony. Those interested in homeopathy will know the hemp agrimony as a medicine for the cure of jaundice, to clear the kidneys and the bladder.

1 *Leave the edge of South Walsham Broad (Viewpoint A), go past the car park and turn left, through a hedge, into a field corner. Follow the left edge and, at the end of a cottage garden, turn left and immediately right along the edge of another field to a lane.*

2 *Turn left and, just past a cottage, turn right into a green track. Follow to a lane and continue to Fen cottage (Nature Trail entrance) and then on to a road junction.*

3 Two mile (3.2km) walk: *turn right and go to point 7.*
Six mile (9.7km) walk: *turn left in a farm road to farm buildings and continue into a green track to a field by an iron hurdle.*

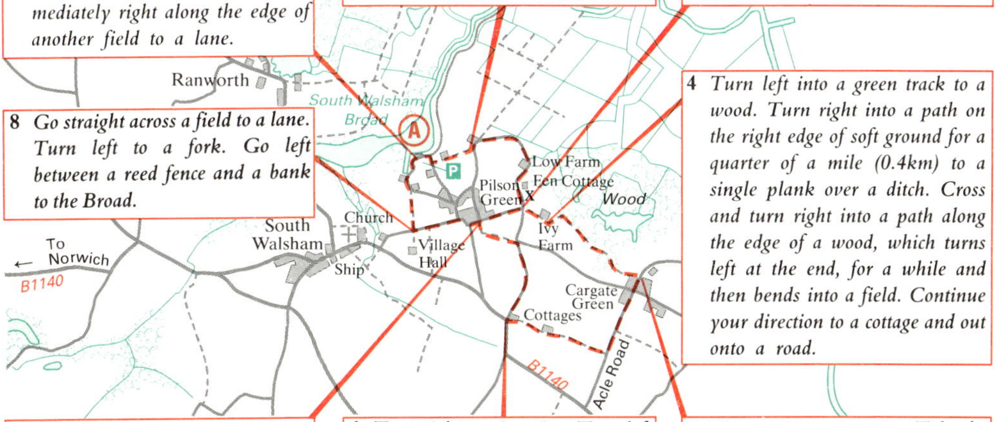

4 *Turn left into a green track to a wood. Turn right into a path on the right edge of soft ground for a quarter of a mile (0.4km) to a single plank over a ditch. Cross and turn right into a path along the edge of a wood, which turns left at the end, for a while and then bends into a field. Continue your direction to a cottage and out onto a road.*

5 *Turn right to a junction. Take the Acle Road to a wood and, after one more field, turn right into a track on the edge of the next field. Follow to cottages. Continue in the lane ahead to a junction with a road on a corner.*

6 *Turn right to a junction. Turn left through a field gate into a field and cut its right corner to a bank. Cross and continue your direction to another low bank. Turn right, keep the bank left until you reach a road and then turn left.*

7 *Continue to a junction. Turn right for South Walsham and pass a junction, heading towards the village hall. Turn right over a stile.*

8 *Go straight across a field to a lane. Turn left to a fork. Go left between a reed fence and a bank to the Broad.*

Walk 24

BERNEY ARMS AND HALVERGATE MARSH

8 miles (12.9km) Moderate; good shoes or boots recommended

The walk can begin at the moorings on the river Yare (1) or the Berney Arms Halt (10) or on the marsh road from Halvergate (5), Grid ref. 433067, where cars may be safely parked.

The Broadland landscape is unique with its rivers, its wide flat marshland and its long history of management by cattle farmers, reed cutters, wherrymen and fishermen. As described in the Hobhouse Report (1947) ...

'Slow rivers creep between its fields and fens. Shallow meres, called Broads, lie along their courses with edges merging into reed beds or waterlogged alder carrs. The bank of a dyke is an eminence whence you may see white or gaily coloured sails of boats progressing mysteriously across a meadow; you will also see a few scattered woods, a derelict windmill or two, an immense stretch of sky ...'

A Looking across the Halvergate Marsh, we can see that this landscape quality remains. In addition, Berney Mill is restored to working order and a wherryman's pub stands near the confluence of the Yare and Waveney. Some isolated farms also add to the scene.

The outstanding ecological interest lies in the range of plant, insect and bird life found in the region. This particular area, associated with the tidal river Yare, has a different character from the valleys of the Bure and Ant and different again from those at Hickling Broad and Horsey Mere.

This sensitive habitat is now protected by a special government scheme. As we can see, near the Berney Sluices, some of the drained marsh has been converted into arable land served by concrete roads. The progressive effect of such conversions make us shudder.

B As we walk clear of that area, back among the pastures, the fens and under the wheeling birds, life seems good.

Over

Walk 24
Berney Arms and Halvergate Marsh continued

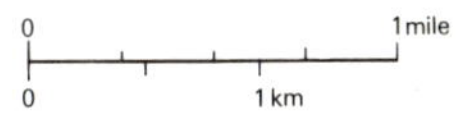

3 *Go through. Pass between two farms. Continue past a derelict mill and, near the next mill, go closely past hawthorns for 1½ miles (2.4km), ignoring all left or right turns, to white cottages.*

2 *Cross a railway into a concrete road. Bend left, then right and, a few yards before a deep ditch, turn left into a faint track. Follow for three quarters of a mile (1.2km) to a gate.*

4 *Go left behind the cottages for half a mile (0.8km) to a junction with another track.*

5 *Opposite the junction, go through a gap lined with rough fencing into a green track. Keep the ditch on your left and, shortly before arriving at a derelict mill, turn right over a bridge into a field.*

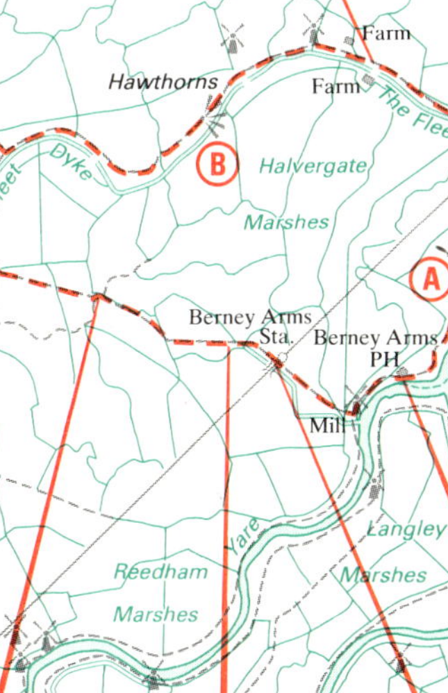

6 *Turn left and follow the ditch on your left round the field to another bridge. Cross and go a few yards towards a gate. Then cross the right hand fence into a field.*

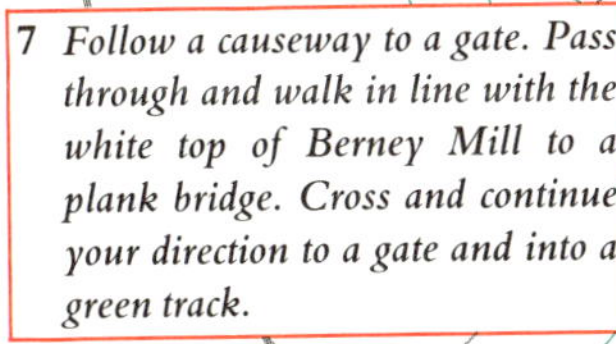

7 *Follow a causeway to a gate. Pass through and walk in line with the white top of Berney Mill to a plank bridge. Cross and continue your direction to a gate and into a green track.*

1 *Leave the Berney Arms on your left and follow the bank to the Berney Sluices.*

8 *Turn left and, after a short distance, turn right into another field. Use the mill to guide you to another gate. Pass through and continue your direction to a ditch which you keep on your left until you arrive at a footbridge.*

9 *Cross and turn left to a gate. Pass through and turn right to a level crossing.*

10 *Go over the level crossing and through gates to Berney Mill, then left on the bank to Berney Arms.*

Walk 25

MARTHAM BROAD

5 miles (8km) Moderate; strong shoes recommended, shorts unsuitable

The walk may be started from Martham village (1) or Martham Staithe (6).

Most Broads are fringed by reed beds, some to a very large extent. Few Broads have unhindered views from their edges like Filby or South Walsham. Visitors must not, therefore, imagine that a walk in Broadland is a Wordsworthian stroll by rippling water. On the contrary, their walk will be among waving reed or sedge with shadows from the clouds moving swiftly across; a glimpse of small ponds and, occasionally, a great expanse of shining water. There will be alder and hawthorn and silver birch. Above all, there will be that special East Anglian light, enhancing colour and movement in the same way that inspired the 19th-century water colourists, called the Norwich School: Crome, Cotman and their contemporaries.

A The path around Martham South Broad is one of the most enjoyable in Broadland: it has wide reed beds from where the boom of the bittern can be heard a mile away and swallowtail butterflies among its many tortoiseshells and other varieties.

Among its bird life, which the extensive reed beds encourage, there are bearded tits performing acrobatics in their whirring flight. Only the male has those striking black moustaches and black undertail. They are seen only in the south-eastern tip of England and when you hear their distinctive twanging 'tching' and their squeaky 'cheen', a moment's patience will give a privileged sight. Throughout the year, marsh harriers hunt over the reed beds.

The village of Martham has some good 18th-century houses around two greens and a fine church. Within the church interior, there is 15th-century glass in the aisle windows. Modern restoration of the hammerbeam roof and carved angels makes a fine sight which is completed, for those who enjoy Victorian Gothic, by the inventive restoration within the chancel.

Over

Walk 25
Martham Broad
continued

1 *From Black Street, Martham, leave the church on your right and go to a junction. Turn right and walk a short way before turning left, through a kissing gate into a path.*

2 *Go ahead into a field. Turn right for a few yards and then turn squarely left. Proceed straight across the field to a bank. Continue to a stile. Cross and walk ahead to a kissing gate, then past a pond to a white field gate.*

3 *Pass through to follow a track through a farm and, immediately clear of farm buildings, turn left and continue to a road.*

4 *Turn right to a stile on the right of a dyke near Martham Staithe.*

5 *Cross and follow a track to a gate. Pass through, over a bridge, and keep to the left of ponds to go up on the dyke bank. Continue to the River Thurne.*

6 *Turn right for half a mile (0.8km).*

7 *Follow the bank, which soon bends right and, after a while, bends left with a view of South Martham Broad. Ignore all paths to your right and follow low wooden rails into a carr.*

8 *Follow a path through bushes which bends away from the Broad and turns left along the edge of the carr to a stile.*

9 *Cross the stile and follow a bank to a wide dyke. Turn right to a swing gate. Pass through and turn right into a green track which narrows to a path past a garage and out to a road.*

10 *Turn left and, just before a junction, turn right into a field. Follow the right edge to a corner. Pass through and rightwards over the next field to a corner of a bank. Pass through and follow another right edge to a barn.*

11 *Follow a clear track ahead to a junction and turn right, past a youth hostel, to another junction.*

12 *Turn left to another junction. Turn right for a while and left into Black Street.*

Walk 26

FILBY BROAD

2 miles (3.2km) Easy; strong shoes recommended

Cars may be parked at Burgh St. Margaret Church (1)

A There is nothing in Norfolk quite as beautiful as the open view across Filby Broad from the path on its west bank. Filby, Ormesby and Rollesby, which are the Trinity Broads, are not connected to any main river in the great complex of Broadland. As a result, most of the holiday traffic has no way of sailing into the Trinity Broads. The great stretch of water is, therefore, ruffled only by the wind and the variety of birds that feed undisturbed upon its surface.

The waters of the main rivers are enriched by nitrates from the effluents of houses and factories and this affects the natural growth along their banks. The reeds and yellow iris on the banks of Filby are, therefore, of a special quality among the glory of Broadland.

The Trinity Broads were not formed by a broadening of the river in the way that most others were and from which the term, Broads, arose. The Trinity Broads were existing Saxon peat excavations naturally filled by the sea. In Roman times, the whole area between Burgh Castle (Walk 15) and the ruined fort in Caister (Grid ref. 517123) was an estuary called Gariensis. Another entry from the sea was through Horsey where the sea each winter threatens to break in again and flood the low lying land of the basin in which the Trinity Broads were formed.

B Burgh Common is a beauty spot of carr and reedbed. In summer, acres of waving sedge, reedmace and dogrose, among many varieties, form a riot of movement and colour. Marsh pea and the great water parsnip can also be found by the enthusiast. In summer, yellow wagtails, reed bunting and sedge warbler feed on the Common while, in the winter, hen harriers and the short-eared owl may be seen.

1 *Start from the east end of Burgh St. Margaret Church. Cross the A1064 onto a footpath. Follow it into a field and along its left edge, then along the right edge of the next field to a cottage. Bend left, then right and cross a stile into a road.*

2 *Turn right and, just past a cottage on the left, turn left in a gravelled path. Follow it to Burgh Common. Turn left in cart tracks which bend right and then turn left and into a hedged track. When the track ends, go past cottages to the marsh verge.*

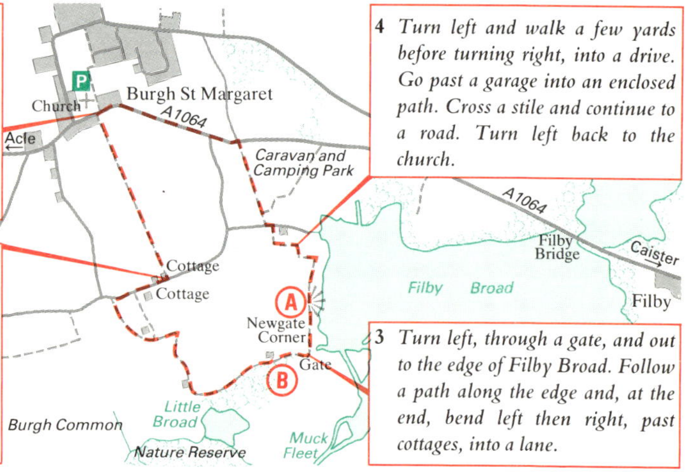

3 *Turn left, through a gate, and out to the edge of Filby Broad. Follow a path along the edge and, at the end, bend left then right, past cottages, into a lane.*

4 *Turn left and walk a few yards before turning right, into a drive. Go past a garage into an enclosed path. Cross a stile and continue to a road. Turn left back to the church.*

Walk 27

BELAUGH FROM COLTISHALL GREEN

4 miles (6.4km) Easy

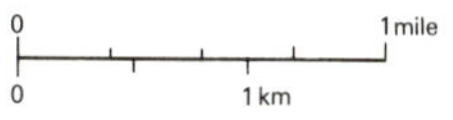

The walk may start at the car park on Coltishall Green, or from the moorings (**1**).

Norfolk was a Parliamentarian stronghold in the Civil War 1642-1646 when a zealous puritan wrote 'The screen in Belaugh Church hath Twelve Apostles, their faces rubbed out by a godly trooper'. Well, so it has, which is rather a pity because the paintings are otherwise very clear.

A Belaugh Church stands on a hill over a well wooded valley of the Bure. The view from its south door, with the river below, followed by a walk through the tiny riverside village, is a perfect delight. As we leave arable fields for a marshland path, great oak trees mark the route.

B Cattle graze along the path and a notice to 'Beware of the Bull' is sometimes displayed. It is unlawful to graze a dairy bull in a field that has a footpath going through. Beef bulls are permitted to graze with cows and are considered safe. If you doubt it, go into an adjoining field and keep your peace of mind. Such notices are usually bluff but a glance over a herd will soon reveal a mighty shape and you can choose your course of action.

1 *Turn right from the car park for the full length of Coltishall Green, then past houses to a junction. Turn left, for Wroxham, to a crossroads.*

2 *Cross, heading for Tunstead and, when the road bends sharply right, go ahead into a green lane. Follow to a road.*

3 *Turn right to a junction. Turn right and walk straight on, between hedges, to another junction.*

4 *Turn left and, immediately over a level crossing, turn right for Wroxham. Go past a farm and fork right, into a track, to a railway bridge.*

5 *Pass under the bridge and bear left with the track to its end in a field. Continue your direction along the left edge to a corner. Turn right for 30yds (27m) to a stile on the left.*

6 *Cross into another field and walk along its left edge to a road. Turn right for a quarter of a mile (0.4km) and then left for Belaugh.*

7 *Follow the road and, at the second junction, turn right to the church. Continue in the low road through the village to a stile on the left.*

8 *Cross the stile and walk over a field to a gate. Pass through into a farm road and turn left. When it bends right, go ahead into a grassy path to a stile.*

9 *Cross and go right, over a marsh. Then walk along its right edge to a stile. Cross the stile and follow more right edges to a double gateway and out onto a road.*

10 *Follow past cottages and a road junction back to the Green.*

Walk 28

HORSEY MERE

4 miles (6.4km) Easy; wet in places, strong shoes

The walk can be started at the car park by Horsey wind pump or the moorings.

Horsey wind pump has been restored to working order and is open to the public during the summer. From its top, there is a splendid view of the surrounding countryside.

Much of the character of Broadland is due to the practices of reed-cutting, grazing and draining. The staithe by the mill is a landing place for thatching reed and has been used for 150 years. During the winter months, reeds are cut on the enormous bed of Brayden Marsh which once, no doubt, was part of the mere. Boats bring the reeds to the staithe for stacking and a ready market.

A The public footpath around the containing bank of the mere has been given a diversion to be used at certain times of the year for conservation reasons. Nevertheless, the path along the boat dyke and the edge of the mere, before you reach the diversion, is a good one.

The mere is a site of Special Scientific Interest because of its wide range of plant and animal life and many good examples can be seen. Among the rare birds which have turned up on Horsey Mere are the osprey, black terns, gadwell, bitterns and Montague harriers. The Mere is regarded as a stronghold for the marsh harrier and strenuous efforts are being made to keep it so.

B In the distance is the high sea wall which protects this low-lying area. Behind it, the sea can be heard rumbling and growling. In Roman times, this area was part of a great estuary and, before the serious floods of 1938 and 1953, the sea flowed in regularly until the high sea wall was built.

Horsey village is a charming little place and its 12th-century church is worth a visit. With the summer traffic flowing by, it is difficult to imagine the utter isolation the village endured until quite recent times. The only roads came across the marshland and were virtually impassable in winter. So isolated was the area, that a camp for French prisoners of the Napoleonic wars was suggested here as a difficult place from which to escape.

Over

Walk 28
Horsey Mere continued

1 *From the windpump on Horsey Staithe, follow the bank and bend left to the edge of the mere.*

2 *Turn right and follow the path to a boathouse, with the mere to your left. Go past the boathouse and turn left, with the bank, towards a diversion sign.*

3 *Go down the bank to a bridge. Cross it and walk left over the marsh. Cross five more bridges back to the bank once more. Turn right to a long straight dyke.*

4 *Turn right to a derelict mill. Turn right to wooden rails and cross into a field. Follow the right edge to a fence. Go through and continue to a corner. Turn left and proceed for 100yds (91m) to a plank bridge.*

5 *Cross the bridge and go past a plantation to a road in Horsey Corner. Turn right for a few yards and turn left, into a drive past a bungalow, to a field.*

6 *Turning left, go round three edges of the field into a road. Follow the road to All Souls Church.*

7 *Turn left to a junction and go right, to the coast road. Turn right for half a mile (0.8km) to the staithe.*

Walk 29

BECCLES

8 miles (12.9km) Moderate; strong shoes recommended for the river banks, shorts unsuitable

There is ample car parking and mooring for boats at Beccles.

Beccles Church is a large Gothic structure overlooking the River Waveney. An octagonal tower, built much later, stands some distance from the south east corner of its chancel and has a peal of 10 bells. The town is a handsome one with a good market place.

Standing on a hill, the town commanded the river in ancient times and became a busy port which sea-going ships could reach. Its prosperity may be assessed from the many Georgian houses and also from the Inns dating from Tudor times. From the footpath on the opposite bank of the river, the gable ends, above walled gardens, are a most satisfying scene.

A Roos Hall, on the edge of Beccles, is a small Elizabethan mansion overlooking the Barsham Marshes. Its setting, among willow trees, and its mullions, twisted chimneys and gables are evocative of its period. It needs little imagination to see the falconer stepping out with hawk on glove to hunt wildfowl over the wild flat scene. The name belongs to the long-departed de-Roos family, whose fortunes were mady by Sir William de-Roos, Knight Banneret to Edward I in his Welsh campaigns.

In summer, as you walk along the marsh path to 'The Locks' public house on the Waveney, the air is filled with the song of larks.

The small pub, on an island in the river, was once busy with wherrymen working their way up the Waveney through a series of Locks to Bungay. The remains of Geldeston Lock, shaped to fit the Wherries of the early 19th century, is a piece of industrial history. In those days, before MacAdam and Stephenson, great efforts were made, at considerable expense, to improve the transportation of goods for the Industrial Revolution.

Over

Walk 29
Beccles
continued

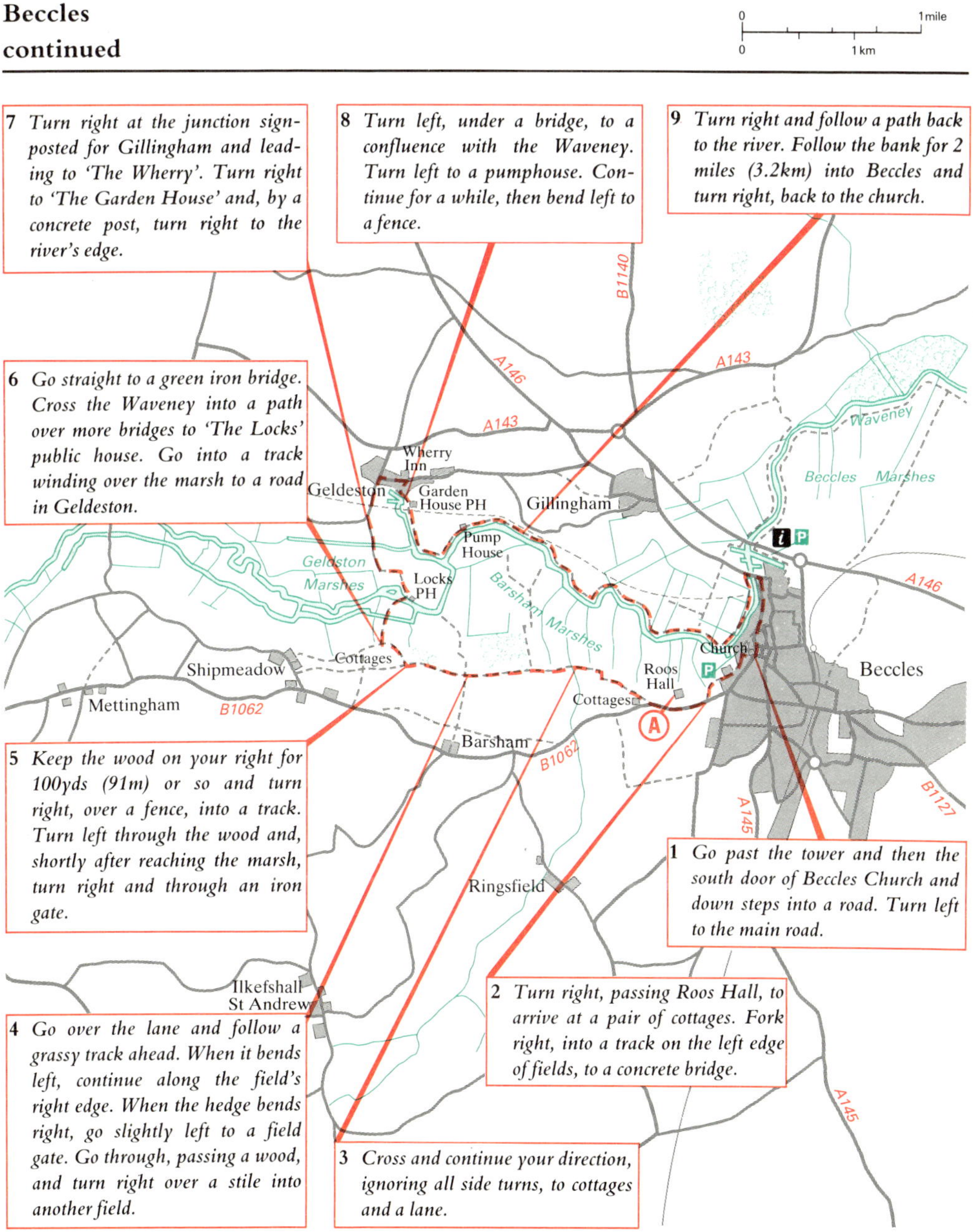

0 1 mile
0 1 km

1 *Go past the tower and then the south door of Beccles Church and down steps into a road. Turn left to the main road.*

2 *Turn right, passing Roos Hall, to arrive at a pair of cottages. Fork right, into a track on the left edge of fields, to a concrete bridge.*

3 *Cross and continue your direction, ignoring all side turns, to cottages and a lane.*

4 *Go over the lane and follow a grassy track ahead. When it bends left, continue along the field's right edge. When the hedge bends right, go slightly left to a field gate. Go through, passing a wood, and turn right over a stile into another field.*

5 *Keep the wood on your right for 100yds (91m) or so and turn right, over a fence, into a track. Turn left through the wood and, shortly after reaching the marsh, turn right and through an iron gate.*

6 *Go straight to a green iron bridge. Cross the Waveney into a path over more bridges to 'The Locks' public house. Go into a track winding over the marsh to a road in Geldeston.*

7 *Turn right at the junction sign-posted for Gillingham and leading to 'The Wherry'. Turn right to 'The Garden House' and, by a concrete post, turn right to the river's edge.*

8 *Turn left, under a bridge, to a confluence with the Waveney. Turn left to a pumphouse. Continue for a while, then bend left to a fence.*

9 *Turn right and follow a path back to the river. Follow the bank for 2 miles (3.2km) into Beccles and turn right, back to the church.*

Walk 30

UPTON STAITHE TO THURNE MOUTH

5 miles (8 km) or a 2-mile (3.2km) short-cut. Difficult/easy; uneven walking on river banks; strong shoes recommended, shorts unsuitable

You can start from Upton Staithe car park (1) or the mooring on Upton Dyke.

On Upton Fen (Grid ref. TG 379137) there is a nature trail developed by the Norfolk Naturalists Trust. Their office at 72, The Close, Norwich will provide full details. Access is free and the Fen is open all year from the gate between Fen House and Fen Cottage.

Before this walk, if you have time, a visit to an area isolated from the enriched river system and fed by clean spring water will be an educational experience. Orchids, honeysuckle and milk parsley, among the reeds where butterflies of many sorts feed, will enliven your interest in Broadland.

Thurne Mouth is a most attractive part of the Broadland Landscape. Northwards lies the passage to the great Broad at Hickling, the Heigham Sound, and the smaller area of Horsey Mere and Martham Broad. Westwards, the Bure and the Ant broaden into peat diggings from earlier times which gave the name of 'Broads' to the lakes and ponds which formed there.

A This is an excellent sailing area where the wind, unhindered over miles of open country, fills the sails of the boats. To the south and west is the typical Broadland landscape of mills and pastures dotted with black and white cattle: wide marshes divided by dykes and connected by flat bridges with enough curves and bends on their lop-sided gates to fill an artist's sketch book.

In the distance is the woodland carr surrounding Upton Broad. Eastwards, low hills and farmland surround Thurne Church. The hole in the church tower for signals to St. Benet's Abbey is described in Walk 31.

B Leaving the green lane and walking across the marsh gives a view unique to Broadland. Boats seeming to sail mysteriously across meadows appear and disappear in irregular procession in a special light under wide skies. By such scenes, a school of painting was inspired called the Norwich School, led by Crome in the 19th century. Your knowledge of Norfolk will be exquisitely enhanced by a visit to Norwich Castle Museum in Norwich where there is a special gallery for paintings of the Norwich School.

Over

Walk 30
Upton Staithe to Thurne Mouth continued

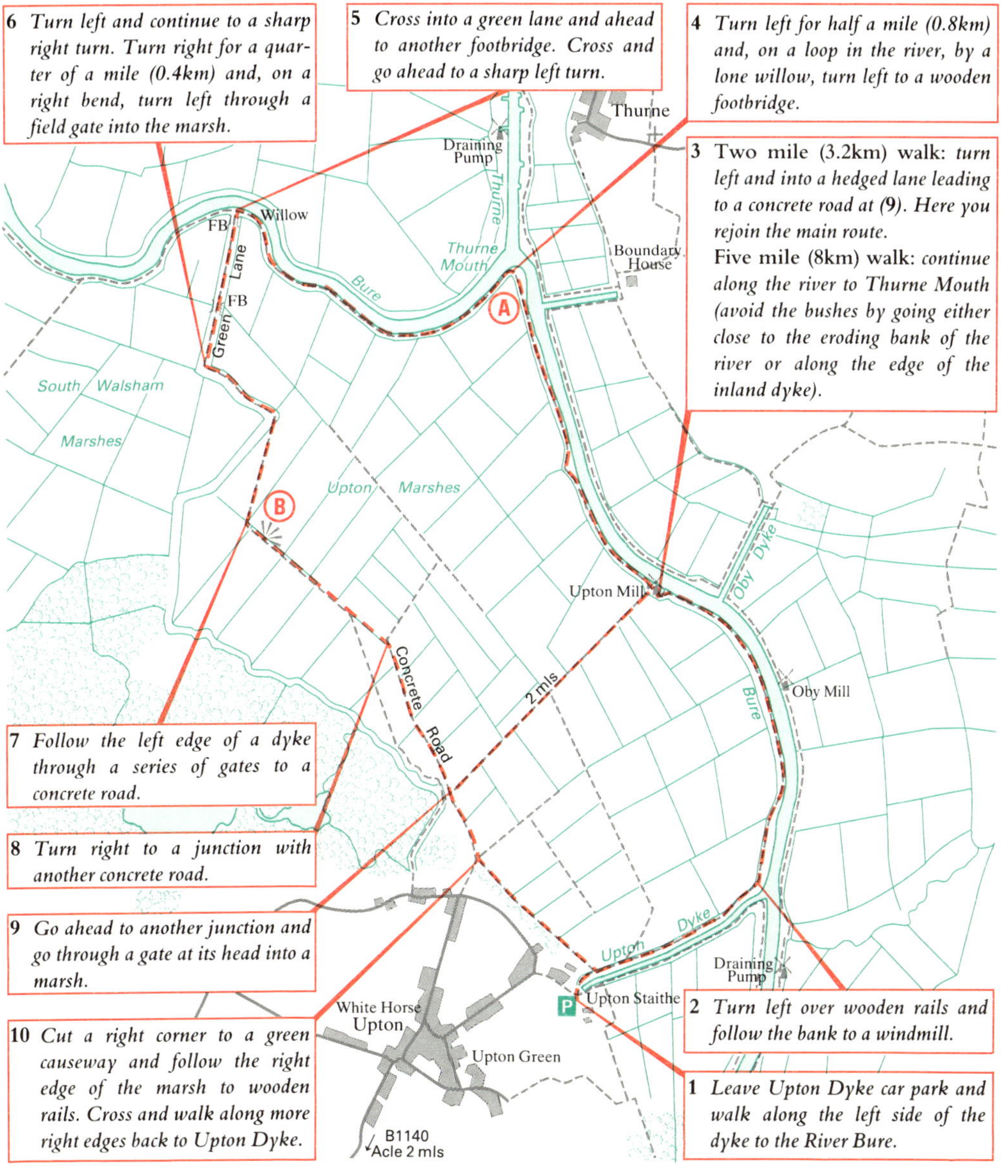

1 *Leave Upton Dyke car park and walk along the left side of the dyke to the River Bure.*

2 *Turn left over wooden rails and follow the bank to a windmill.*

3 Two mile (3.2km) walk: *turn left and into a hedged lane leading to a concrete road at (***9***). Here you rejoin the main route.*
Five mile (8km) walk: *continue along the river to Thurne Mouth (avoid the bushes by going either close to the eroding bank of the river or along the edge of the inland dyke).*

4 *Turn left for half a mile (0.8km) and, on a loop in the river, by a lone willow, turn left to a wooden footbridge.*

5 *Cross into a green lane and ahead to another footbridge. Cross and go ahead to a sharp left turn.*

6 *Turn left and continue to a sharp right turn. Turn right for a quarter of a mile (0.4km) and, on a right bend, turn left through a field gate into the marsh.*

7 *Follow the left edge of a dyke through a series of gates to a concrete road.*

8 *Turn right to a junction with another concrete road.*

9 *Go ahead to another junction and go through a gate at its head into a marsh.*

10 *Cut a right corner to a green causeway and follow the right edge of the marsh to wooden rails. Cross and walk along more right edges back to Upton Dyke.*

Thurne
Draining Pump
Thurne
Willow
FB
Green Lane
FB
Thurne Mouth
Bure
Boundary House
South Walsham Marshes
Upton Marshes
Upton Mill
Oby Dyke
Concrete Road
2 mls
Bure
Oby Mill
Upton Dyke
Draining Pump
Upton Staithe
White Horse
Upton
Upton Green
B1140 Acle 2 mls

Walk 31

THURNE CHURCH

5½ miles (8.9km) Easy; good shoes

The 14th-century tower of the Thurne Church has a circular hole driven through its wall on the west side. Through it, St. Benet's Abbey can be seen 1½ miles (2.4km) away (Walk 7). There is a belief that, when sickness occurred in the locality, a light would be placed in the hole in order to summon the monks who were wise in the use and preparation of medicines. Help would be sent for the afflicted via the Bure and Thurne in those days before a health service. This system ended when Henry VIII reduced the Abbey's power and united it with Norwich.

Those who enjoy legends may be interested in one that still persists of a ghostly light that shines from Thurne Church whenever there is illness in a wife or child in a marshman's lonely cottage.

A During the walk on these mild uplands among the farms, the view is over flat marshland dotted with windmills. The River Thurne, winding through the middle distance is a route through which almost every holiday maker will pass at some time in craft hired by the week. In summer, the water is thronged with motor boats and the scene is one of relaxation and gaiety. In winter, more serious enthusiasts tack and wear their graceful sailing craft in a fierce game against tidal currents and biting wind.

In the autumn, a great variety of wildfowl fly in to spend the winter on the Broads and marshes. The expert will enthuse over the tarsus and mandibles of an identified specimen but the casual walker of more romantic nature is captivated by the bright red feet and bill of a rare merganser. This red breasted bird plunges its bottle-green head below the surface as it pursues a fish. Its chestnut, black and white plumage is quite distinctive among the bird life of Thurne, adding extra interest to the colour of the river scene.

Over

Walk 31
Thurne Church continued

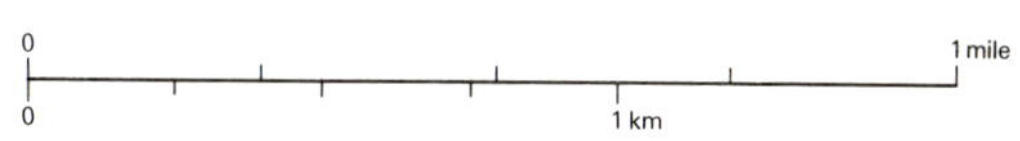

1 *From Thurne Staithe, turn left at the Red Lion for half a mile (0.8km) to a junction. Take a 'No Through' road ahead, which turns right, to a caravan site.*

2 *Go ahead into a green lane, past three scattered cottages to a field gate, on your left, near a farm. Turn right, over a dry ditch, into a field. Go a few yards ahead and then along the right edge to a wooden post. Turn right and turn left, along the edge of a field to a road.*

3 *Turn left. Continue for a quarter of a mile (0.4km) and turn right, into a green lane bordered with power poles, to another road.*

4 *Turn left for a short distance and then turn right in another road to a junction.*

5 *Turn right and then left, at a post box, to a farm. Continue for a short distance and bend right into a concrete road to another farm.*

6 *Leave the concrete road and pass to the right of farm buildings. Turn left, at their rear, to a fence. Turn right and, when the fence bends left, go in line with Thurne Church to a road.*

7 *Turn left at the road and, opposite a hedge corner, turn right. Cross a field under power lines to another hedge corner. Turn left and continue for a short distance before turning right into a path to Thurne Church.*

8 *Take the green lane on the left of the church into a field. Go along left edges of fields over stiles to a concrete road. Turn left, winding through a farm, to a road in Thurne and turn right to the staithe.*

Walk 32

NORWICH RIVER AND MOUSEHOLD HEATH

4 miles (6.4km) Easy; good shoes recommended

A visit to the Norfolk Broads should include a visit to the fine city of Norwich. There is an abundance of moorings by the yacht station near Thorpe station and car parking is rarely a major problem.

As mentioned in several walks in this guide, Norwich Castle Museum is a treasure house both of the natural history of Norfolk and of the Norwich School of painting. The exhibits are skilfully presented and will greatly enhance the visitor's knowledge of the Broads. There is also a rural life and industrial museum in Bridewell Alley nearby which vividly recounts the story of windmills and Norfolk life.

A There is a glorious view of Norwich Cathedral from the bank of the Wensum.

B Above the city is Mousehold Heath, a wild place conserved for the local people as a place of recreation. The story associated with the Heath is of Robert Kett, who led a revolt against land enclosures in the 16th century. His rebels successfully held the heights until, forced to descend for food and water, they were scattered by mercenary troops under the Earl of Warwick.

Norwich ranks among the most pleasant of cities to visit. Its shops, restaurants and entertainment are of the highest and most up-to-date standard but Norwich has also preserved enough of its past to give a flavour of grace, antiquity and learning. The tourist office in the ancient Guildhall is a fount of information.

Over

Walk 32
Norwich River and Mousehold Heath continued

1 *Start at the 'Compleat Angler' on Foundry Bridge, opposite the yacht station. Go down steps to the river bank. Continue to Pulls Ferry and then along the bank to a road.*

2 *Cross the road and continue past a cow tower into a path which leads to a road by the 'Adam & Eve'. Continue your direction to Palace Plain. Turn right and over a bridge to a roundabout.*

3 *Turn right and walk a short distance before turning into Silver Road. Go uphill to a Baptist Church and turn right into Mousehold Avenue.*

4 *Follow the avenue to a pavilion on the edge of Mousehold Heath. Turn left into Gilman Road.*

5 *After a short way, turn right into a dip and follow a wide path into a valley to another road. Turn left. After a short distance, fork left into a clear footpath. Follow to a triple fork and take the centre path to the Ring Road.*

6 *Turn right to crossroads and continue ahead to a sports ground. Turn right in a track to the end of fencing and turn right, then left at once, into a path on a bank. Continue your direction to a crossing path into a valley.*

7 *Cross to a path ahead and wooden posts. Follow a rough road to its end and turn left, then left again into Britannia Road.*

8 *Follow the road to a clock tower at Britannia Barracks. Turn right and go over the Heath to the Mottram Memorial, then down the ridge to a road.*

9 *Turn left to a roundabout. Turn right for 100 yards (91m) into Barrack Street and cross into a gravelled lane to the river. Follow the left bank to steps. Go up to a road past Bishop's Bridge and ahead to Foundry Bridge.*

Walk 33

BUNGAY AND OUTNEY COMMON

6 miles (9.7km) Easy; strong shoes recommended

The river is navigable to Bungay and car parking is not a problem.

Bungay is a picturesque and pleasant town with a ruined castle which belonged to the mighty Roger de Bigod. He overlorded Norfolk in Norman times and once defied King Stephen whom he called 'the King of Cockney'. King Stephen stormed and took the castle and it was demolished.

In the market place, a Butter Cross with a leaded dome was built in 1690 after the great fire in 1688 which destroyed the whole town. The town was rebuilt with wide and handsome streets from its market place to the principal roads. As might be expected for such an important river crossing, traces of Roman and Danish settlements and the ruins of a Norman Priory have all been found here.

A Outney Common is a fine pasture covering about 400 acres (162 hectares), skirted by the Waveney in a horseshoe under the Bath Hills. The river provides very pleasant walking along its banks.

The south-facing Bath Hills are a natural sun trap. Spring flowers bloom and nightingales sing earlier on these slopes than anywhere else in England.

Over

Walk 33
Bungay and Outney Common continued

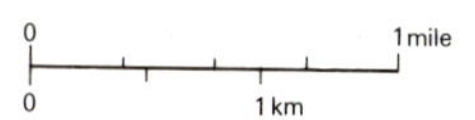

1 *Start in Bungay town centre and go to the right of the 'Three Tuns' to follow Broad Street to its end. Continue over a by-pass in front of you and go ahead into a road through a gate on to Outney Common.*

Follow a track with a wall on your right, and when it ends, turn right and continue with iron rails on the left. Pass through a gate and follow a track ahead, eventually over a plank bridge and through another gate. Go slightly right now to cross a bridge on the far side of a meadow.

2 *Continue over another bridge and follow a path ahead. After 100yds (91m) or so, turn left through another gate and into a drive. Follow the drive for a short distance and then fork right over the verge and uphill through pine trees to a stile.*

3 *Cross and follow the path ahead for a mile, with Outney Common below, to a road by a bungalow. Turn left and continue through a gate to a house and straight on through another gate into a grassy track.*

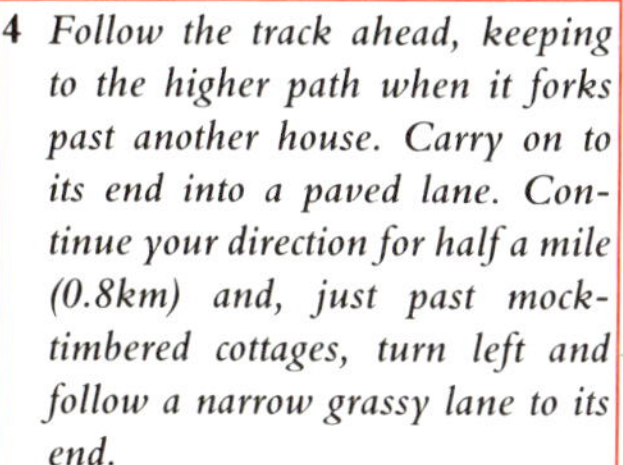

4 *Follow the track ahead, keeping to the higher path when it forks past another house. Carry on to its end into a paved lane. Continue your direction for half a mile (0.8km) and, just past mock-timbered cottages, turn left and follow a narrow grassy lane to its end.*

5 *Turn right into a road and continue to its end by a disused railway station where you turn left to a main road. Go straight over onto a path on the left of a memorial.*

Turn left at the end of the path, soon forking right, to pass close to Earsham Church. Then pass into an unpaved road. Go over a humped bridge and when the track becomes green, continue to a plank bridge.

6 *Cross over and turn left and, keeping as close as you can to the stream, follow its bank to a bridge and a road.*

Turn right and follow the road into Bungay once again.

Walk 34

HORNING

5 miles (8km) Easy; boots or wellies recommended, shorts unsuitable

There is a car park near 'The Swan' (1) and adequate moorings in Horning.

Horning is a large and straggling village with a distinctive Edwardian flavour lent by 'The Swan' public house and by inlets and boathouses on the riverside. Many later Victorians described the Broads and its secret, reedy places and marshes with intense feeling. It was the Edwardians who first organised boating holidays in the bracing air of Norfolk.

The industry has grown until places like Horning, lying between the Ant and the Bure, teem with summer visitors, shopping and stopping for refreshment at 'The Swan' and the riverside 'Ferry Inn' at the end of Lower Street. There is more, however, to this fine old parish than boats, shops and pubs.

A Contrasting with the bustling village are the fertile meadows and marshland paths nearby. Reached by lovely lanes past the fine tower of St. Benedict's Church, they are cool and rich with wildlife. The route through the woodland carr and meadow has been stiled and waymarked by the Broads Authority and presents no problem for even the most casual walker.

The return journey is not always quite so easy because the fields might still be in crop. Experienced walkers never regard such matters as being of great concern but the lightly shod may prefer the quiet lanes.

At the crossroads before you enter the village, you will see one of those remarkable village signs which are so numerous in Norfolk. Local worthies look into the past to find out why early folk should have settled in that place. Based on their findings, ingenuity and craftsmanship are then employed to produce a graphic memorial to the village.

Horning in the saxon tongue means 'folk who live between two rivers'. Canute, it seems, gave the land to the monks of St. Benet's Abbey 4 miles (6.4km) away (Walk 7), who were then most prosperous.

Over

Walk 34
Horning continued

1 Leave the car park near 'The Swan' and follow Lower Street near the river for a mile (1.6km) to a turn signposted for the Ferry Inn (worth a look).

2 Continue in Lower Street into School Road and turn right at the school for the church.

3 Take a footpath on the left past the churchyard and along a field edge to Horning Upper Street (a track on your right leads to some good views over the Bure).

4 Turn left and turn right into Upper Street to the main road. Turn left for 100 yards (91m) or so and turn right in a track next to Grove Cottages.

5 Follow the track over a marsh to a low bank. Continue your direction, with woodland carr on your right and, near a boathouse, turn left over a ditch to the marsh.

6 Go a short way along the right edge to a plank bridge and a stile on your right. Cross and go straight through a carr to another stile. Climb over into a field.

7 Turn left and along the edge of fields to a corner and a line of trees. Turn right and follow the trees and, near a farm, turn left between two posts into another field. Follow the right edge to a stile and into a road.

8 Turn left to a fork. Go left past a dell to an RAF station.

9 A few yards past the RAF entrance, at the head of a farm track, go up a bank into a field corner. Cross the field diagonally to a cream-painted cottage in the distance, or go around the field edges to the same point.

10 Turn left to crossroads and cross straight over back to 'The Swan'.

Walk 35

HADDISCOE MARSHES

8 miles (12.9km) Moderate; boots or wellies recommended, shorts unsuitable

There is a car park in St. Olaves, half a mile (0.8km) from the Haddiscoe Bridge (1) and there are moorings for boats nearby.

A Long tramps over marshes are the essence of discovering Norfolk Broadland and this walk is an introduction to Haddiscoe Marsh and its nearby villages. These are rich grazing marshes with occasional carrs of willow or silver birch. In the distance, there are wooded hills around Thorpe where a peninsula of land to Thurlton juts northwards towards the Norton, Thurlton and Chedgrave marshes.

Over this area, you can see almost every type of bird known to Broadland, including the pheasant, teal, redshank, snipe in the spring, cuckoos in summer and the wild geese which come on short winter days.

These birds no longer arrive in the large flocks and numbers that earlier writers on the scene have recorded. More efficient drainage and use of fertilisers have reduced the conditions and food supplies considerably but determined action is now in progress to restore the traditional scene.

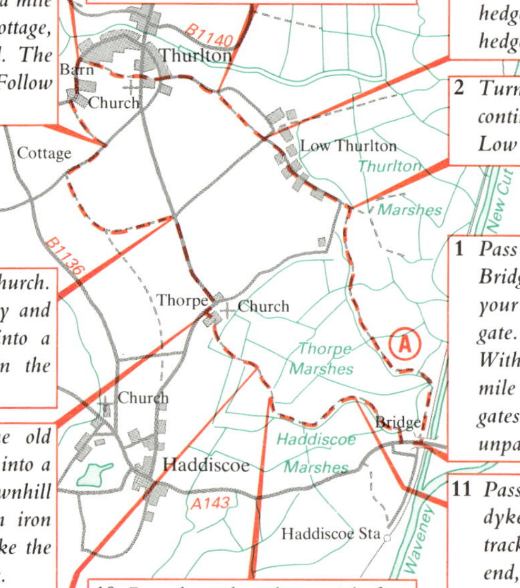

1 *Pass under the Haddiscoe Road Bridge, with the New Cut on your right, and walk to a field gate. Pass through and turn left. With a dyke on your right for a mile (1.6km), pass through more gates to a green lane and out to an unpaved road.*

2 *Turn left to a road corner and continue your direction, through Low Thurlton, to a road junction.*

3 *Cross and go through a gate, by a kiosk, into a field. Go round a depression and follow a hedge to a farm track. Go over and straight down a field, through a gap in the hedge, and continue, with the hedge on your right, to a road.*

4 *Turn left to a junction. Turn right, for a few yards, and left into a path to a church. Cross over into a track ahead, then fork right into a path to a road.*

5 *Turn left for a quarter of a mile (0.4km) and, opposite a low, tiled barn, turn left into a farm track. Follow over two fields to a road.*

6 *Turn right for a quarter of a mile (0.4km) and, just past a cottage, turn left into a farm road. The road becomes a green lane. Follow to a road.*

7 *Turn right to a neat little church. Turn right for a short way and ignore the first opening into a farmyard and turn left in the second.*

8 *Go downhill, past a fine old farmhouse, and fork right, into a marsh road. Continue downhill and bend left, through an iron gate and, after a while, take the right hand of two more gates.*

9 *Continue your direction on the right edge of a dyke and, after a while, follow the ruts leading you to the centre one of three gates.*

10 *Pass through and turn right for a 100 yds (91m), jumping a small ditch on the way, and turn left to follow a dyke on your right into a long curve to a gate.*

11 *Pass through and, keeping the dyke on your right, follow the track which bends right at the end, over a flat bridge to a gate. Pass through and still keep the dyke on your right to another gate. Turn right, through the gate, to the main road. Turn left to the bridge.*